D0251472

Critical Praise for
David F. D'Alessandro

"With its engaging voice and pull-no-punches tone, *Brand Warfare* book stands out from the marketing crowd."

—*Harvard Business Review*

"In this short, concise work, D'Alessandro, CEO of the John Hancock insurance group, entertainingly hammers home the importance of creating and maintaining a brand. In his view, a brand is whatever image a customer conjures up upon hearing a company's name, so everything from the firm's labor practices to its product and advertising must be taken into account. To make his points, D'Alessandro draws heavily on his former career in advertising and public relations. On having Orville Redenbacher as a client: 'We literally thought he was insane.' But in the end, he says, 'Orville taught me...the power of a good brand to trump all rhyme or reason in the marketplace.' ... He succeeds at reminding everyone from the CEO to the people on the assembly line that their company's brand is its most crucial asset. Practical, psychologically astute and clearly written, this book has much to offer businessfolk of all stripes."

—*Publishers Weekly*

"Ready to hit the trenches to defend your brand? David F. D'Alessandro, CEO of John Hancock Financial Services, arms readers with a battle plan in *Brand Warfare.* Drawing on years of experience, D'Alessandro offers 10 tips for nurturing a good brand—that is, one that 'offers comfort, trust, convenience, and identity.' Some basic concepts, including how to manage scandal, will already be familiar to marketing professionals. But D'Alessandro amuses and instructs with his bluntness. For instance, he says that 'survival in the advertising game demands that the agencies learn how to flatter and milk their clients.' Of greatest value to the brand warrior are his discussions of the successes and failures of such well-known outfits as Amazon, Coca-Cola, Nike, and his own John Hancock. And he says branding should aim not only at consumers but also at a company's employees. After all, 'the best people want to work for the best brands.'"

—*BusinessWeek*

"D'Alessandro is that refreshing rarity: a business-man who tells it like it is. And he does just that in his gripping new page-turner, *Brand Warfare.*"

—*Chicago Sun-Times*

"In *Career Warfare*, David D'Alessandro, chairman and CEO of John Hancock Financial Services, offers the unwritten rules of organizational life, the real truths you need to know in order to build the kind of personal brand that shouts 'headed for the top.'"
                                            —*Soundview Speed Review*

"It seems that Mr. D'Alessandro has written this book [*Career Warfare*] mostly for the reason he offers: he has spent more than 30 years at different companies and wants to share his insight to help others develop their career.... 'At the risk of appalling all the humanists out there, I can tell you that it's smart for you to try to think of yourself as a product—an expensive one—because at the end of the day, that's exactly what you are to your organization, to your boss, and to your customers,' he writes. That's a very unchief-executive thing to write. Some advice may seem obvious to people who have already climbed the professional ladder, but the author presents his analysis in such a refreshing way that the reader keeps turning the pages.... All in all, the book offers a refreshing message of humanity from someone who has fought many corporate wars."
                                            —*The New York Times*

"This time [with *Career Warfare*] he narrows the focus, honing in on executives and interpersonal dynamics. With advice and examples of how to differentiate one's personal brand—clearly his area of expertise—D'Alessandro warmly and wittily conveys practical experience, along with his self-effacing skepticism of touchy-feely corporate platitudes."

—*The Miami Herald*

"…It turns out that all of us have personal brands, and we need to manage them with the same care and energy Fortune 500 firms bring to the task. This is the message of *Career Warfare*, the latest how-to book by David D'Alessandro. D'Alessandro's books are short, with plenty of attitude. His last book was called *Brand Warfare*. The repetition of the word 'warfare' is not an accident. For D'Alessandro, the business world is a dangerous place. At any time you can step on a land mine and blow up your career."

—Knight Ridder News Service

"D'Alessandro is far and away the most unusual top executive in town. In a world where you are supposed to tend to the bottom line and stick to the safe center, D'Alessandro was not afraid to be as loud as the loud ties he wears. When Boston janitors went on strike, he was the first to speak up for them. Very early on he wrote an opinion piece calling on Cardinal Bernard Law to quit. The fact that he helped bail out the Boston Marathon by underwriting it with Hancock dollars, so remarkable at the time, is now just one line in an extraordinary résumé chock-ablock with leadership roles at places like Partners Healthcare, the Wang Center and Boston University. Everything he touched he made better."

The Boston Globe

EXECUTIVE
WARFARE

EXECUTIVE WARFARE

10 RULES OF ENGAGEMENT FOR WINNING YOUR WAR FOR SUCCESS

DAVID F. D'ALESSANDRO

AUTHOR OF *BRAND WARFARE* AND *CAREER WARFARE*

WITH MICHELE OWENS

New York   Chicago   San Francisco
Lisbon   London   Madrid   Mexico City   Milan
New Delhi   San Juan   Seoul   Singapore
Sydney   Toronto

2 3 4 5 6 7 8 9 0   DOC/DOC   0 9 8

ISBN   978-0-07-15423-8
MHID   0-07-154423-2

McGraw-Hill books are available at special quantity discounts to use as premiums and sales promotions, or for use in corporate training programs. To contact a representative, please visit the Contact Us pages at www.mhprofessional.com.

This book is printed on acid-free paper.

For Michael, Andrew, and Robert

CONTENTS

Contents

ACKNOWLEDGMENTS

Legendary bluesman B.B. King begins one of his many famous songs with the lyric:

Nobody loves me but my mother, and she could be jivin' too.

The song was not written about career development, but nonetheless contains a valuable lesson for people seeking success in organizational life.

Nobody you work with loves you. If you think they do, you are "jivin'" yourself.

I wrote this book to help people avoid mistakes, think with a clear head, and not get lulled into believing accomplishments are all they really need to get ahead. The higher one goes in any organization, the stiffer the competition. There is little room for "love".

But this is the page where an author thanks the many people who contribute to his work which follows, and I have plenty of affection for all those great folks.

Michele Owens, my coauthor, is brilliant, hilarious, incredibly talented, and I am proud to have worked by her side on three books. She makes the process of book writing a joy. My old friend and sage advisor Steve Burgay always encourages me to press on and convert my history and observations into lessons. Becky Collet, a real star who has worked with me for years, somehow finds the patience to deal with my idiosyncrasies. My assistant, Antoniette Ricci, somehow perseveres through the hectic pace of my life. Amy Hinson is a rare person. She read and reread every word and helped make this book fresher and more contemporary. And where would any author be without a great lawyer like Ike Williams? Mary Glenn, my editor, continues to have faith in Michele and me. She challenges us to keep on point and rise above our previous works.

I also need to thank some of the people I have worked with who taught me by allowing me to watch them in action. I don't believe they would all agree with every one of my interpretations and lessons learned, but without them, I would still be working in my family's delicatessen. Among the most notable are Bob Kleinert, Jack Connors, Jack McElwee, Jim Morton, Steve Brown, Bill Boyan, Mike Bell, Alan Einersen, Bob Marston, and Bob Muir. Then there are the unnamed ones I never liked but learned from anyway.

There are two men, coincidentally both named Dominic D'Alessandro, who deserve my gratitude. My father showed me that the path to success is never straight or predictable—but perseverance has its own reward. The other Dominic, CEO of Manulife Financial, who I am not related to, gave new meaning to the creed "be a man of your word." Now, no person in their right mind thanks his father and not his mother. Rosemary taught me the value of listening carefully and being direct when necessary—even if it caused confrontation.

Lastly, I am grateful to the thousands of characters I have met who, through their brilliance, stupidity, selflessness, greed, honesty, or deceit, wove the fabric of this book.

EXECUTIVE WARFARE

INTRODUCTION

If You Are Not Interested in Success,
Put Down This Book and Buy a Latte

Genius may have its limitations,
but stupidity is not thus handicapped.

Elbert Hubbard

Let me first say that if you are perfectly content in your current job, more interested in scrapbooking or drinking games than in getting ahead at the office, or contemplating life as a cloistered monk, do not buy this book. If, however, you are harboring any thoughts of rising into senior management, read on.

In the early 1970s, when I was in my early twenties, I thought that if I could only reach a point in my career where I would be managing a few people and making the astounding amount of $100,000 a year, I would be as content as if I were lying under a Tuscan olive tree, being hand-fed peeled and seeded grapes.

But that is not what happens, is it? In a few short years, when I actually *was* managing a few people and making $100,000 a year, my definition of success had changed. Instead of basking under the olive trees, I was trying to figure out how to jump the next hurdle.

This is a cycle that all ambitious people understand, whether they work for a university, a nonprofit, a newspaper, a partnership, or a Fortune 500 company. Wherever they are, they want to reach the next level, and it's all they want. Then they get the big promotion that's everything they ever wanted. They grow into the job and start doing well at it, and pretty soon they are looking around saying, "Is that all there is?"

It doesn't matter that they have already outstripped their own early definition of success, their families' and neighbors' definitions, too. They are addicted to climbing the ladder. They just can't help it. And the worst thing that can happen to them in a career is to get stuck.

Yet the truth is, once you reach a certain level, the odds are against your rising higher, and there are more and more people standing in your way.

ONCE YOU REACH A CERTAIN LEVEL, THE ODDS ARE AGAINST YOUR RISING HIGHER, AND THERE ARE MORE AND MORE PEOPLE STANDING IN YOUR WAY.

While I have read hundreds of so-called management, success, and leadership books—some philosophical, some pious, and some just self-aggrandizing—I have not read one that gives any really practical advice for beating those odds and continuing to rise.

Well, I happen to have a lot to say on this subject. In my career, I've had the chance to observe the struggles of smart, talented people trying to break into senior management in dozens of different corporate cultures, as well as at universities, nonprofits, and in government. I began my career in the 1970s in advertising and public relations, and my clients included many of the big forces of the day, such as Gillette, Mobil Oil, and Owens Corning. My employers have also included Citibank and the one-time computer giant Control Data, as well as John Hancock Financial Services, where I became CEO in 2000. In addition, I have served on the boards of many nonprofits.

Along the way, I've seen a lot of people who failed to catch the wind, some who crashed painfully, and others who skillfully gathered the momentum to rise—enough of each to codify a few thoughts about the nature of flight when it comes to careers. While my last book offered advice about getting on the road to success, I wrote *Executive Warfare* for those already successful men and women who are nonetheless intent on moving upward—the ones with the courage, stomach, and desire to break out of the middle of the pack and get to the top.

> **IT'S NO LONGER ENOUGH TO BE SMART, HARD-WORKING, ABLE TO SHOW RESULTS; YOUR RIVALS ARE ALL SMART, HARD-WORKING, ABLE TO SHOW RESULTS.**

The problem is, it's relatively easy to be successful in the middle. You just have to do the things that were drummed into all of us as children: be smart, hard-working, able to show results. Once you reach a certain point, however, it's no longer enough to be smart, hard-working, able to show results; your rivals are *all* smart, hard-working, able to show results. These qualities are like the ante in a

4

high-stakes poker game. Everybody has to pay those dues to play. But a lot of people think that *all* they have to do to win is pay those dues. They are markedly mistaken—and most find this out the hard way and usually too late.

There is also another catch that no one tells you about—not when you're a child, not when you're a college student, not when you're a young and eager employee—not ever, for that matter. It's not just that the pyramid narrows and the competition toughens as you rise. It's that the game changes fundamentally.

At a certain point on the way to the executive suite, the simple chain of command you have worked under for years turns into filigree, and you no longer have just one boss to please. You now have a complex, hazy matrix of hundreds of bosses. And you cannot rise without impressing a good number of them.

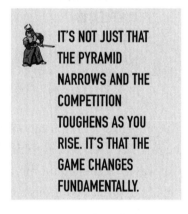

IT'S NOT JUST THAT THE PYRAMID NARROWS AND THE COMPETITION TOUGHENS AS YOU RISE. IT'S THAT THE GAME CHANGES FUNDAMENTALLY.

These bosses include not just your direct boss, but also the people above him or her to whom you have now become visible, including the organization's chief executive and the board of directors. Your other new bosses include every single person who has any influence over any of these higher-ups.

Chances are good that the higher-ups are listening to your peers. They are also listening to the people in human resources, the general counsel's office, and the accounts payable department that processes your expenses. They may very well be listening to some of your underlings, too, who are probably more prominent themselves than any underlings you've ever had to supervise before.

These bosses are definitely listening to the outsiders you might expect to be influential, such as clients, regulators, and the press. But they're also listening to the ones you don't expect: the spouses of the people you work with and the guy at the gym who notices your temper tantrums when you lose a racquetball game.

So now, in addition to getting your job done and done well, you have to develop some very adult skills. You have to manage an incredibly tricky network of relationships, simultaneously, in private and in public, and in a way that announces your ability to lead. The experiences that have brought you to this point can in no way have prepared you for the subtle, tortuous, and sometimes crazy-making challenges you'll now face.

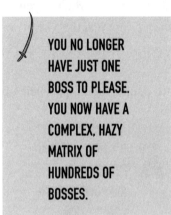

YOU NO LONGER HAVE JUST ONE BOSS TO PLEASE. YOU NOW HAVE A COMPLEX, HAZY MATRIX OF HUNDREDS OF BOSSES.

This I learned on my third day with the title of vice president. I'd just come to John Hancock as an outsider to run the company's communications. In John Hancock's 122-year history, I was the first vice president ever hired directly from outside the ranks.

It was a big step up for me, and the way I was treated was pretty heady stuff. I was given a gorgeous big office on one of the top floors of the beautiful building Henry Cobb of I.M. Pei & Partners had designed for the company on Boston's Copley Square. Soon, people were arriving with stylish design plans and asking me questions like, "Do you prefer to furnish with antiques or something more contemporary?"

What I'd *been* used to was this: When you took a new job, whatever furniture was in the office when you got there was your furniture. And if there were any delay in your moving into that office, most of the good stuff would have been pilfered by the people in the neighboring offices.

Of course, I didn't understand that just because I'd now have an office fit for a prince, that didn't mean that a few offices over, there weren't half a dozen other princes and princesses thinking very hard about how to block me, use me, or kill me.

In my new position, I was assigned a whole series of people, and I was on my best behavior meeting my new employees, including one woman who came from Thailand. Let's call her Mali.

I'd just been to Thailand for the first time and had really enjoyed the trip. "Bangkok is a beautiful and fascinating city," I said to her. "Incredibly industrious, wonderful food, intriguing history. . . .

"I took a tour along the river," I went on in an outpouring of friendliness, "which I really loved, except for the polluted river itself. You must be proud to be from a country with such a unique culture. . . ."

Mali smiled at me and was very animated, and we had a great conversation.

The next thing I knew, I was having the opposite kind of conversation with my new boss—a very unhappy one.

"Mali says she can't work for you," he informed me, "because you have no empathy for her ethnic origins."

"But I told her I *loved* her country," I protested.

"Look, it doesn't really matter what you said. What matters is, she thinks you said she comes from a dirty country, and we don't want this to escalate up to the president. So I'm taking her department away, I'm taking it away now."

> YOU HAVE TO MANAGE AN INCREDIBLY TRICKY NETWORK OF RELATIONSHIPS, SIMULTANEOUSLY, IN PRIVATE AND IN PUBLIC, AND IN A WAY THAT ANNOUNCES YOUR ABILITY TO LEAD.

I was dumbfounded. I hadn't even had my company physical yet, and I'd already lost a whole department. If the *Guinness Book of World Records* had a contest for "fastest loser of a department," I would have won—hands down.

What had happened was this: There was somebody else at John Hancock who wanted Mali's department, and he resented a newcomer taking it over. So when Mali told him that I'd called a polluted river "polluted," he saw an opportunity to stir up doubts about me in my boss's mind—and seized on it.

I'd been there three entire days. I had no idea that I even *had* rivals. And this was in genteel old Boston, at an old-line company where if you got in, you got in forever. The John Hancock of that era made the Civil Service culture look cutthroat. However, I was like a foreign bee that had invaded a long-standing hive, and the other bees were going to do something about it.

 I DIDN'T UNDERSTAND THAT JUST BECAUSE I'D NOW HAVE AN OFFICE FIT FOR A PRINCE, THAT DIDN'T MEAN THAT A FEW OFFICES OVER, THERE WEREN'T HALF A DOZEN OTHER PRINCES AND PRINCESSES THINKING VERY HARD ABOUT HOW TO BLOCK ME, USE ME, OR KILL ME.

That same unpromising week, one of John Hancock's executive vice presidents invited me to lunch. Before we'd unfurled a napkin, he said to me, "The senior officers are taking bets, you know."

"About what?" I asked.

"About how long you're going to last. There's actually a pool. They're giving ten-to-one odds that you don't last six months."

"How's it going?"

"So far, no one's bet for you."

I looked at him. "How did you bet?"

"I make my bet," he said dryly, "after the lunch."

Even at the time, I thought that was pretty funny of him, and I laughed.

He bet against me anyway. And lost, because I went on to run the company, and he eventually worked for me.

I'm actually grateful for that harsh introduction to John Hancock. It taught me a few essential lessons about what it means to move into higher management—and fast. That nobody gives you a honeymoon period.

That good intentions do not count. That every foolish word out of your mouth is now subject to scrutiny by the people both above and below you. That there is so much at stake—money, prestige, the power to make real decisions—that the competition will be ruthless. That bosses at this level will not put up with anything or anybody who risks embarrassing them. That this is a new game called hardball, and the problem is, you can strike out without even seeing a pitch.

When you are promoted to senior management, my advice is to celebrate the night before you start the job, because there is no celebrating afterward. Just because you've been made a field general and given a spiffy new uniform with epaulettes doesn't mean that you won't have battles to fight.

You'll now have to impress that complex matrix I mentioned earlier, everybody from the commander-in-chief to the lowliest private, from the other generals to the Pentagon correspondent at the *New York Times*. And you can't always expect to be judged fairly.

Some of these people will know you intimately. They may well have worked with you for years. In any case, you've moved into a smaller orbit near the top of the organization. The trouble with that, of course, is that familiarity can breed contempt, and people may discount your hard work and dedication just because they are in the mood for a new face.

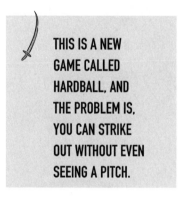

THIS IS A NEW GAME CALLED HARDBALL, AND THE PROBLEM IS, YOU CAN STRIKE OUT WITHOUT EVEN SEEING A PITCH.

Even worse, some of these people will be actively rooting for you to fail. There are your peers, a much smaller group now, some of whom will benefit directly if you go down in flames. There are also those people with nothing to gain, who simply enjoy a crash scene if they stumble across it. Of course, if it's a nuclear event for the organization, that's one thing. But a nuclear event for your career? Don't kid yourself. A lot of people will not mind that at all.

Consider the case of publisher Judith Regan. Her career at Harper-Collins ended in late 2006, thanks in part to the controversy surrounding her acquisition of what many viewed as a confessional book by O. J. Simpson. Regan had brought so many successful books to HarperCollins. You'd think that when she was fired, her coworkers would, at a minimum, have mourned the loss of future revenues. Instead, there was no shortage of them willing to share their glee with the press.

SOME OF THE PEOPLE JUDGING YOU WILL INEVITABLY BE MEAN, POWER-MAD, INCOMPETENT, OR JUST PLAIN CRAZY. I'VE SEEN PEOPLE IN ALL KINDS OF SENIOR MANAGEMENT JOBS THAT I WOULDN'T ALLOW TO LITTER-TRAIN MY CAT.

And let's admit the truth: Some of the people judging you will inevitably be mean, power-mad, incompetent, or just plain crazy. I've seen people in all kinds of senior management jobs that I wouldn't allow to litter-train my cat. And yet they were responsible for hundreds or thousands of careers.

As you go along, you may also find it very difficult to measure your own success. At a certain level, your bosses cease giving you praise when you do well. High performance is simply expected. And when you do badly, you now have enough power of your own that you probably won't be killed off directly, unless you do something truly offensive, like date the boss's spouse. Now it's a matter of how many dents you take. You'll take some unavoidably, but you can't take too many—and how many are too many?

You may find it difficult to assess your performance even by your own standards. For most of your career, you've almost certainly succeeded by being an expert of some kind or other—engineer, tax specialist, community organizer, professor of anthropology—and by managing small groups of people on projects you've understood better than anybody else. With a move into higher management, however, you're suddenly thrust into a new role, one where you are now managing experts in fields you have no knowledge of. It's a case of the blind leading the sighted, and if that role fails to alarm you, you're either too full of yourself, too immature, or just too plain stupid to be successful.

And when you move up, you'll be represented by people whose names you barely know because you no longer have six or ten people working for you. You now have a hundred or a thousand or five thousand. Yet the quality of your hiring decisions—and the hiring decisions of the people you've hired—looms large as people judge your ability to lead.

What's more, you may well find yourself being blamed for problems that you had no part in creating simply because you are the person now in charge. In organizational life, they *do* sometimes kill the messenger.

Finally, you may find yourself struggling with geopolitical turmoil—redrawn national boundaries or your old commander-in-chief ousted and replaced by a stranger—while you're in the midst of battle.

For example, it's been virtually impossible in recent years to pick up the business pages of any newspaper without seeing scandal after scandal breaking: books cooking, options backdating, lying to Wall Street, lying *on* Wall Street, plus the ever-popular personal peccadilloes story. Every one of these scandals represents career upheaval for more people than you might guess. Even more career plans are thrown off track by mergers and acquisitions and dislocations in the economy, such as the one set in motion by the subprime mortgage crisis.

IN ORGANIZATIONAL LIFE, THEY DO SOMETIMES KILL THE MESSENGER.

And in an information age when a single careless comment can live on in infamy, even nonprofits and universities are no longer the calm, secure berths they once were. In late 2005, University of Richmond President William E. Cooper was done in by a moment of excessive honesty when he complained that, given the quality of his student body, his institution was only "turning mush into mush." Soon after, he announced that he'd be stepping down.

You don't have to flame out yourself, either. Have a boss who flames out, and you may soon follow him or her out the door. You can be rising happily within an organization for two decades, only to find the rug pulled out from under you in an afternoon.

As a result, the very worst thing that can happen to you if you intend to climb is to develop a sense of entitlement just because you've been somewhere for a long time. You may think, "Look, I've put my 15 years in, I've come through six jobs, I deserve this next job." Well, the world does not work that way anymore. It's no longer useful to have a ten-year plan. Even God had only a seven-day plan.

THE VERY WORST THING THAT CAN HAPPEN TO YOU IF YOU INTEND TO CLIMB IS TO DEVELOP A SENSE OF ENTITLEMENT JUST BECAUSE YOU'VE BEEN SOMEWHERE FOR A LONG TIME.

So you'd better develop the ability to improvise above all.

And the higher you go, the more nimble you have to be. Consider this little statistic: According to Joe Griesedieck of recruiting firm Korn/Ferry International, 40 percent of CEOs fail within their first year or two on the job. There are species of fruit flies with longer life expectancies. I wrote this book not to alleviate the uncertainty that comes with any move into higher management, but rather to alert you to the things you *should* be worried about—and what to do about them.

In my experience, the single greatest reason why otherwise talented people get stuck in midcareer is because they believe that the same rules that applied for the first part of their career still apply. They don't. You now have to master a much subtler set of rules.

You'll need to learn how to acquire the global perspective your peers lack, when and how to deliver bad news, when to take a shot at your rivals and when to be gracious, and most important, how to handle the many new influences on your trajectory.

In *Executive Warfare*, we'll take those influences one by one—including bosses, directors, underlings, peers, and clients—and show you how to deal with them in a way that will get you where you want to go.

Intelligence, imagination, and cunning are all required here—but not underhandedness. You know, thanks to my earlier books, I'm sometimes accused of being too manipulative and Machiavellian in my view of organizational life. That was not true of those books, nor is it true of this one. I don't believe that you need to be devious to succeed. In fact, I think that being excessively political is a mistake. I also don't advise turning yourself into a heartless machine. If you have no humanity, you will inspire no one. And no matter how tough the game gets, you are more likely to win it if you maintain your sense of fun.

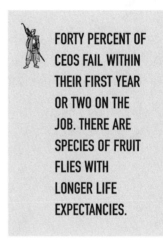

FORTY PERCENT OF CEOS FAIL WITHIN THEIR FIRST YEAR OR TWO ON THE JOB. THERE ARE SPECIES OF FRUIT FLIES WITH LONGER LIFE EXPECTANCIES.

That said, you *do* have to be aware of your surroundings.

Defense at this level is largely about trying to figure out where the ball is going. And you are certain to run into some very manipulative people. If you fail to anticipate what the other players are doing, you are not a player. You are why they invented bleachers.

Learn to play this game, however, and the rewards of reaching the top of an organization are more than worth the trouble. The difference between being a vice president and a senior vice president can easily be hundreds of thousands of dollars a year for many years. It can be the difference between actually making the kinds of decisions you've always

 **INTELLIGENCE, IMAGINATION, AND CUNNING ARE ALL REQUIRED HERE—BUT NOT UNDERHANDEDNESS.**

dreamed about making versus merely participating in them.

You will have to take risks to rise, and you will make mistakes. I've made plenty, and I'll share them with you. Through triumphs and stumbles, the essential thing is to make it clearer and clearer to the people around you that you ought to be in charge.

This book will tell you how to lead all your many bosses to the inevitable conclusion that you, and you alone, have what it takes to run the show.

ATTITUDE, RISK, AND LUCK

They Are the Most Influential Bosses

Most people would rather die than think; in fact, they do so.

Bertrand Russell

I don't care what your parents told you. You can't be anything you want to be. Some people simply cannot play the piano well, no matter how hard they try. Some people will never succeed as investment bankers, either.

Even among those people who do play the piano well, very few will get to Carnegie Hall. On the other hand, a substantial number of them could conceivably make a good living at a piano bar. The same holds true in every kind of career. Most businesspeople will never be invited to run General Electric. But that doesn't mean they can't become rich and famous at a solar panel startup or old-line fabric house.

Much of life—and work—is about finding the right instrument to play in the right orchestra. Sounds easy? It's not.

I figured this out early. Like most public school kids of my era, my musical education started with the flutophone, which is basically a baby clarinet without a reed.

Then, in fourth grade, it came time for the kids in my class with any degree of talent or non-talent to join the school band. So we each got an appointment with the head of the music department, Mr. Wetzel.

Mr. Wetzel asked me, "Well, David, what instrument do you want to play?"

Excitedly, I said, "I really want to play the clarinet." This was the natural next step after the flutophone.

"We don't have any more clarinets," he said. "All the clarinets are gone."

"That's okay," I responded cheerfully. "Then I want to play the saxophone."

> MUCH OF LIFE— AND WORK—IS ABOUT FINDING THE RIGHT INSTRUMENT TO PLAY IN THE RIGHT ORCHESTRA.

He shook his head. "You can't play the saxophone unless you play the clarinet first."

I thought. A trumpet is like the clarinet because you blow through it, and it has keys and stuff. Besides, it's kind of a cool instrument. After all, Louis Armstrong played one. "What about the trumpet?"

No, the trumpets were taken. At the end of the day, I couldn't even get a stringed instrument like a cello or bass or even a drum. Yes, I had a choice—tuba or trombone—but I had never even seen either one up close before.

I reluctantly chose the trombone. But two years later I asked again for a clarinet. Mr. Wetzel's answer was, "Well, you can't have a clarinet because you've already been playing the trombone for two years. You're a sixth grader now, and we have fourth graders who get the clarinets."

So I played the trombone for six years, hated every moment of it, and learned that life is not fair.

Most careers are a lot like playing in Mr. Wetzel's orchestra, and I don't care if that career takes place in a giant corporation or in the priesthood. Most people know they want to play some instrument, but they are not sure that the instrument they've been handed is the right one. So they end up in jobs that aren't necessarily suited to their best skills. They may not even know what their best skills are because they haven't been developed yet. Possibly the orchestra itself is not very sympathetic to them and has given them no chance to find out where they could really shine.

There are a million reasons why people become trapped in the wrong place with the wrong job, but my point is that most of them do become trapped. They might have picked the wrong major in college or took an entry-level job in the wrong field because that was all that was available at the moment. Maybe they graduated with a fine arts major but succumbed to pressure to join the family business buying wholesale lots of nuts and bolts and have hated their working lives ever since. Maybe they stayed in a city with few opportunities because their spouse didn't want to leave.

EVEN INCREDIBLY SMART PEOPLE END UP MERELY DOING WELL BECAUSE THEY BECOME UNWILLING TO RISK ANY CHANGE.

Even incredibly smart people end up merely doing well, but never getting to play in a bigger arena, because their personal lives have locked them into place, and they become unwilling to risk any change.

When I was young and working in New York, for example, I knew a guy who was Jackie Gleason's personal publicist. He wanted to move into network television. He was brilliant and creative, and I'm sure that he would have been terrific there. However, when I asked him why he didn't get into television, he shrugged. "The TV networks don't look in the public relations direction when they're looking for executives. And I can't afford the pay cut I'd have to take for an entry-level job." He was only in his mid-30s, but as far as he was concerned, it was already too late.

Meanwhile, all the people like him, trapped in the wrong jobs, are quickly surpassed by the lucky few who are in the right jobs, those people with a natural aptitude for the profession in which they find themselves.

Having a natural aptitude for an instrument is such an enormous advantage that if you don't have it, you have to work three times harder than the people who do, even to be credible. And you may never be more than mediocre.

> HAVING A NATURAL APTITUDE FOR AN INSTRUMENT IS SUCH AN ENORMOUS ADVANTAGE THAT IF YOU DON'T HAVE IT, YOU HAVE TO WORK THREE TIMES HARDER THAN THE PEOPLE WHO DO, EVEN TO BE CREDIBLE.

The shrewdest thing you can possibly do is to spend your 20s questioning whether you have the right instrument in the right orchestra and making your way there. If, however, like most people, you reach midcareer without even having explored a change of instruments—and you find that you are not rising—you don't have to do what most people do, which is resign themselves to their own frustrated ambitions.

Sure, it may be too late for you to become an astronaut or a ballerina. But I don't believe that successful careers are necessarily about following a childhood dream. What matters is finding a job for which you are well suited, one that makes you happy. And that *is* doable.

WITHOUT LOSING OR COMPROMISING YOUR JOB, IT'S POSSIBLE TO LEARN ABOUT OTHER AREAS OF YOUR OWN ORGANIZATION AND WORK YOUR WAY INTO A POSITION WHERE YOU'RE THE ONE WITH THE NATURAL APTITUDE WHO CAN PLAY RINGS AROUND THE OTHER MUSICIANS.

Without losing or compromising your job, for example, it's possible to learn about other areas of your own organization, make contributions there, figure out what you like to do, and work your way into a position where you're the one with the natural aptitude who can play rings around the other musicians.

If your organization is run by a Mr. Wetzel, and God forbid that someone who joined in percussion should ever play the flute, it's also possible to move to a different kind of organization where they really don't care *where* you started as long as you can do something valuable today.

For example, I entered John Hancock in communications. I'd worked in public relations and advertising, and I was using the instrument I'd been handed. But what I really liked was marketing, which is much more sales-, price-, and product-driven. I knew that John Hancock happened to need good marketers, so I seized the opportunity to learn a new instrument and trade in the old one. Soon, I was playing the right instrument in an orchestra that was glad to have me. Eventually, they made me conductor.

To rise, you too may have to broaden your horizons, and you may have to look for an employer who will allow you to broaden them. You'll also need three things to make the most of the chances you are given: the right attitude, a willingness to take calculated risks, and dumb luck.

Let's take these deciding factors one at a time.

ATTITUDE: The Boss Within

It's incredibly important to get your own head in the game if you intend to rise. If fear or sloth rules your psyche, you'll never do what you need to do to stand out from the crowd. If you are bossed around by your own greed, arrogance, or childish lack of discipline, you will give people reason to doubt you, and you will undermine yourself.

Let's talk about a handful of things you need to do to appear to be material for higher management.

First, though it sounds obvious, learn how to present well. Meetings are the stage on which you rise or fall, thrill or flop—so make sure that you know how to express yourself there. Quietly take lessons, if you need to, at your own expense.

Second, study, study, study. Not to master your own art, not to master the art of knowing what everybody else knows, but to master the art of knowing what nobody else has even considered.

I used to make sure that I had a staff person who spent a lot of time analyzing the company I worked for as a whole, helping me to understand what was really going on in all the areas outside my own. And I would be briefed, three times a week, on their major initiatives.

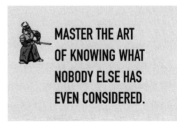

MASTER THE ART OF KNOWING WHAT NOBODY ELSE HAS EVEN CONSIDERED.

That way, if something came up in a meeting, I'd be prepared. For example, I once learned that my company was thinking about investing in a joint venture with the Colombian government. So I put in the time required to learn about the political climate in Colombia.

During the meeting at which this idea was presented to the top decision makers, I asked, "What happens to our investment if the guerillas destabilize the government or a civil war breaks out?"

This was a question that needed to be asked, but the people whose job it was to ask it had not thought about it. My bosses suddenly looked at me as if I might be the most valuable person in the room.

By learning as much as you can about the organization as a whole, you are able to show dimension and prove that you belong in a broader role—possibly one that spans the whole organization.

There are other, smaller ways of showing dimension, too. I once had a boss who was dying to go to Wimbledon. This was long before the advent of eBay made buying tickets to anything easy. None of my peers could figure out how to get him there, but I could. Now, was that going to make me the person who went up to the next job? No, but it was not going to hurt, either.

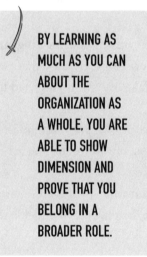

BY LEARNING AS MUCH AS YOU CAN ABOUT THE ORGANIZATION AS A WHOLE, YOU ARE ABLE TO SHOW DIMENSION AND PROVE THAT YOU BELONG IN A BROADER ROLE.

You will have to do many other things that we'll talk about in subsequent chapters, such as hire well, motivate your employees, and convince your boss to trust you. Ideally, you will bring in truckloads of money for the company or partnership or university and get to a point where people start thinking they cannot afford to lose you.

Most important, you will have to not be stupid. This sounds obvious, but I have seen so many cases of ridiculous stupidity even at the highest levels of organizational life that perhaps it is not so obvious.

The first thing people are told when they go into politics is, "Get used to the scrutiny." This applies just as well to higher management. You are being judged every minute, and small things can tip the balance in your favor or against it.

Let me give you an example. I was once in one of those general stores you find in small Vermont towns that have everything. This store had a little restaurant, made sandwiches to go, and sold coffee mugs, sweat shirts, and canned tomatoes. I went to check out, and near the box of maple-sugar moose candies by the cash register, there was a board with Xeroxes of people's driver's licenses and the checks they'd bounced.

And I saw one of my own employees there. It wasn't a very big check, something around $37.90. He wasn't a criminal, obviously.

But every time I saw that guy after that—or glanced at his name on a list of possible promotions—I thought, how responsible can he be?

THE FIRST THING PEOPLE ARE TOLD WHEN THEY GO INTO POLITICS IS, "GET USED TO THE SCRUTINY." THIS APPLIES JUST AS WELL TO HIGHER MANAGEMENT.

Virtually everybody in business is supposed to have some knowledge of how things work financially, if only to control their own budgets. Fail to pay your child support or have your wages garnisheed by the IRS, and your chances of being promoted even at the most senior level go out the window.

You can't allow your own aggressive tendencies to make you irresponsible, either. There are a lot of Type A personalities in senior positions, and they're very, very competitive in everything they do. I mean, they play croquet competitively.

I can remember an incident from a conference I attended many years ago that was one of the stupider things I've ever witnessed. A tennis game was scheduled, mixed doubles, with the CEO's wife and another executive's wife playing against two senior managers, one of whom we'll call Charlie.

The two women were decent enough tennis players, but the men were much stronger. What should have been a friendly game turned into a fiercely competitive one. Instead of gauging his serve to the skill of his opponent, the polite thing to do, Charlie was using his best serve on the CEO's wife, and she simply could not return it.

He was just vicious, to a point where a ball bounced up and ended the game by injuring her eye.

That night, I was at the CEO's table for dinner. Charlie came by to apologize to the wife, who had more than her usual amount of makeup on. She was quite good about it. She laughed and said, "Oh, don't worry about it."

The CEO only said coolly to him, "I hear you have quite the serve, Charlie." The rest of us at the table knew what that meant. That meant, "Your life in this company is over."

YOU CAN'T ALLOW YOUR OWN AGGRESSIVE TENDENCIES TO MAKE YOU IRRESPONSIBLE.

It takes a lot of discipline to make it to the senior levels of any organization and a tremendous amount of discretion, not just in your professional behavior but also in your personal behavior.

I highly recommend that you keep your personal life private. Take the risk of people not knowing you. Anything you do reveal, trust me, will eventually come back to haunt you.

For example, high on the list of life's unfairnesses is contracting a serious illness. Even more unfair is the fact that if you contract a serious illness, you have to hide it if you possibly can. I know very few people who've ever been promoted after a heart attack. Never mind that bypass surgery is a miracle. A heart attack is a showstopper, particularly if the job you want to be promoted into is considered "stressful." And it's a question of odds.

The decision makers, who have choices, tend to think, "Why take a chance on somebody who has had a heart attack? Because if he or she dies within a couple of years, I'll look stupid. Why should I look stupid?"

For precisely the same reason, nobody who admits to being an alcoholic gets to be CEO. You may get big bucks in your career, but you don't get the big chair. So, if you have a drinking problem, by all means keep it to your off-hours and conceal it.

Conceal it even if you don't have a problem. My theory is that if somebody sees you with two tumblers of scotch in the same night, it's problematic. Despite the great popularity of large martinis, you should never have a martini at a company event. Ever. Once you embarrass yourself in public, you will never get rid of that aura of doubt.

The same is true if you distract people with your messy sex life. Let me tell you a story. One day, I came back from lunch and passed by a woman waiting in my foyer. Let's call her Brenda. She was the secretary of a senior executive who worked for me—we'll call him Oscar—and she was crying.

I said to my secretary, "What does Brenda want?"

My secretary shrugged. "She says it's an emergency, and she has to talk to you."

So Brenda came in and told me that she was sleeping with her boss. Which, by the way, I could have cared less about. The company had no nonfraternization rule. It was highly discouraged, but it was not against the rules.

However, since she was weeping and choking and sobbing to the point that I was scrambling for Kleenex, I had to address the situation.

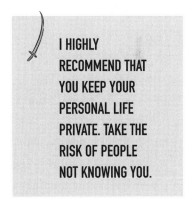

I HIGHLY RECOMMEND THAT YOU KEEP YOUR PERSONAL LIFE PRIVATE. TAKE THE RISK OF PEOPLE NOT KNOWING YOU.

I was very careful not to pry. I said, "If you are filing a sexual harassment complaint, we'll call Personnel right now, and they'll come and interview you. If that's not the issue, this is just something you and Oscar have to work out."

She said, "I don't know what to do. I love him so much."

And now Brenda's starting to pour her heart out to me. The affair has been going on for three or four years. She's so in love. But Oscar is rejecting her because of another woman in the office, who's an executive, not a secretary.

It turned out that Oscar was not only in the middle of a nasty divorce, but also sleeping with two coworkers at the same time. It was like *Big Love*, the HBO show about polygamy, except that I didn't think there was any "living the principle" here. This was more "unprincipled living."

I didn't want to seem cold, but the last thing I wanted was to be involved in was this quadrangle. I now know that I have to call the law department to look at the financials to make sure that Oscar is not using company money on either of these women. And I'm not happy about it.

So, after Brenda dried her tears and left, I called Oscar to my office. We were not friends, but I knew him well. He came in, all smiling.

I said, "You are not going to believe what happened to me after lunch today. Brenda came to see me."

His smile fell.

"I don't need to know any details, but are you having a relationship with another woman, too?"

He said, "Yes. I'm trying to get rid of Brenda."

"How is she going to go away? She's your secretary. She sits twelve feet from you every day. And this other woman marches in and out of your office a dozen times a day.

"Personally," I said, "I don't care. But what are you, stupid? This is going to be a mess now."

So he told me that he would take care of it.

A week went by. I came back to my office from a meeting, and sitting in my foyer is somebody new. The executive Oscar's been sleeping with. Angry as a hornet.

Oscar had decided that the way to solve this problem was to erase the blackboard. So he dumped both of them. And the executive was now furious with *me*, convinced that her ouster from Oscar's affections was my fault.

I didn't want to punish the women in this case, so I had the lawyers work out transfers for the secretary and the executive. They actually wound up in better jobs. But Oscar? He had gone from somebody who was going places to a mere curiosity.

The truth is that there are always office romances. People spend a lot of time together, it happens. There is no illusion that everybody in the workplace is a saint, and everybody makes mistakes. But there is a big difference between playing with matches and doing what Oscar was doing, which was walking a tightrope over a volcano.

THERE ARE ALWAYS OFFICE ROMANCES, BUT THERE IS A BIG DIFFERENCE BETWEEN PLAYING WITH MATCHES AND WALKING A TIGHTROPE OVER A VOLCANO.

And be aware that even the most benign and above-board office romance has consequences. Make sure of your ground before you make any kind of romantic overture to a coworker because you're changing the dynamic forever, one way or the other. If it turns into a relationship that's really going, one of you is probably going to have to leave. If it doesn't, it will be very hard to maintain the same collegial relationship you had in the past.

With every office romance, somebody is going to move on faster than natural laws would dictate. So think about whether it's worth it.

CONFORMITY IS NOT A PREREQUISITE FOR POWER

You have to be discreet in your personal behavior to rise, but you don't have to be a conformist. Every ambitious person is going to take some knocks. If you try to fit the mold of your organization too much, the rap will be that you are too dull or too dry or too sycophantic. So you might as well be yourself and get points for having the courage of your own style.

Although I was as ambitious as the tip of a blue flame, by the time I reached John Hancock, I did not even try to fit in. I tried to avoid company-sponsored social events as much as possible. With some of my superiors, this didn't sit well. They thought I was arrogant, standoffish, not a team player.

But it wasn't about arrogance. It was about the fact that things would be said at dinner that people would regret the next day, and I'd rather not risk either hearing or saying something stupid.

I was also much more direct than many of the people I worked with, and my bosses occasionally gave me trouble about it.

And I certainly did not look the part at John Hancock, an old-line Boston company dating back to 1862. My ancestors came from the Basilicata region of Italy, not the Back Bay. When I started at John Hancock,

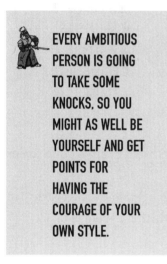

EVERY AMBITIOUS PERSON IS GOING TO TAKE SOME KNOCKS, SO YOU MIGHT AS WELL BE YOURSELF AND GET POINTS FOR HAVING THE COURAGE OF YOUR OWN STYLE.

the uniform was an off-the-rack suit from Brooks Brothers, a blue Oxford shirt, and the same striped tie. I would have felt like I was wearing a costume in those clothes. So I wore Italian suits and bright ties.

When I looked around the Hancock boardroom, there were seven or eight oil paintings of the former CEOs. Most of them looked like our country's founding fathers, Alexander Hamilton types with sharp profiles, swept-back hair, and impressive cravats. In no way did I resemble those people. I actually once said that to the CEO when he was giving me a promotion: "I'm very happy for the promotion, but I have no illusions that my picture is ever going to hang on that wall."

He said, "Don't be so sure about that."

The first hint I had that style questions wouldn't hold me back came from the most unlikely person, a distinguished old Brahmin named Elliot Richardson, who was on the board of John Hancock. Richardson had had an illustrious career in government, serving in cabinet positions under

Richard Nixon and Gerald Ford. He'd also shown considerable personal courage during the Watergate scandal, when he was attorney general. Nixon had ordered him to fire Watergate special prosecutor Archibald Cox. Richardson refused, resigning instead.

At John Hancock, we used to have lunch together as a board, and one afternoon Richardson and I both came in late. Everybody else had wandered off, so for the first time, it was just the two of us sitting at the table. Richardson had just gone to his fiftieth reunion at Harvard and said conspiratorially to me, "You know, if a guy was an ass at 21, he's still an ass at 71."

I thought that was very funny. Then Richardson went on to say, "Most people don't know this about me, but one of my ancestors was a quarter Italian," as if this made the two of us Sicilians in arms.

It was not only amusing, I thought it was quite endearing. It was his way of telling me that as far as he was concerned, I was okay. And for the first time I understood that I could be a contender for the top job at John Hancock.

I'd advise you to be yourself, but also to disarm potential critics where you can by being self-deprecating.

In my case, since I was much more aggressive and direct than my peers and wore ties with so much more wattage, I think it was extraordinarily important for me to maintain a sense of humor. If you'd have taken away my sense of humor, then there would have been no question that I was just an ambitious jerk.

Humor has helped me deflect many an awkward question over the years, including at the press conference in Toronto in 2003 where we announced that John Hancock was merging with the large Canadian insurer Manulife Financial. When a reporter asked me why I was paid more than most Canadian CEOs, there was only one possible answer.

"America is a great country."

Everybody laughed, and we left it at that.

RISK: Slice It, Dice It, and If It Looks Good, Eat It for Breakfast

One of the most significant attitude adjustments you will have to make as you move into higher management is your attitude toward risks. If you have played it safe thus far in your career, understand that you can no longer avoid taking risks—big ones, where the stakes are frighteningly high. On the other hand, if you've been a rambler and a gambler, you can no longer afford to be entirely freewheeling, either. Higher management is all about handling risks intelligently and in a calculated fashion.

BE YOURSELF, BUT DISARM POTENTIAL CRITICS WHERE YOU CAN BY BEING SELF-DEPRECATING.

For example, we've recently come out of a period when mortgage lenders were extending credit to virtually anybody, devising subprime loans that allowed many people to get into the housing market way over their heads. Clearly, there was going to be a backlash to that kind of exposure, and nobody should have been surprised when there was a tsunami of foreclosures in 2007.

But the CEOs of some of the world's most sophisticated financial organizations apparently didn't see it coming and made big bets on securities based on these subprime mortgages because they generated outsized fees and returns. Charles Prince of Citigroup, E. Stanley O'Neal of Merrill Lynch, James Cayne of Bear Stearns, and Peter Wuffli of UBS all lost those bets, were forced to write down billions in late 2007, and lost their jobs.

In other words, these executives took on too much risk, which does more to end careers than anything except taking on too little.

Even if you never have to deal with the kind of quantitative risks that Wall Street uses to make its living, risk is still the name of the game. If you work in a nonprofit, you may someday have to decide whether to accept a big donation from someone who has been indicted or, worse, who gets indicted after you take the gift and spend it. If you manufacture art supplies, you may have to decide whether to move into the children's craft market. Thousands of jobs may hang on your decision, not to mention the forward movement of your own career.

Let me tell you about a moment when I was unwillingly forced to bet the house.

I'd taken over John Hancock's retail division in 1991, a huge step up for me. I'd hardly been there six months when I found myself in the midst of a decade-old problem that was about to boil over. For the last 10 or 15 years, a number of salespeople throughout the life insurance industry had been taking advantage of their customers in two ways.

First, some of them were rolling over existing insurance policies with a cash balance into new policies for one purpose only—to generate commissions. In some cases, the customers didn't even know they were being rolled over because the documents were forged.

The second problem was salespeople selling life insurance on the basis of "vanishing premiums." The idea was that because the customer's premiums were invested in the stock market, there would be a point at which the premium bills would vanish and the life insurance would be paid for out of investment returns.

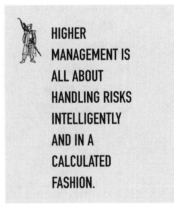 HIGHER MANAGEMENT IS ALL ABOUT HANDLING RISKS INTELLIGENTLY AND IN A CALCULATED FASHION.

This was sold aggressively as a way to have life insurance without having to worry about the cost as you grew older. Our sales presentations virtually guaranteed vanishing premiums. Then the stock market stopped cooperating, and customers began getting bills they'd never expected. And if they didn't pay, the only thing that would "vanish" was their policies.

There was plenty of blame to go around for this stuff. Fortunately, though, it did not fall on me and my team, since we were new. Life insurers had clearly either not put sufficient checks and balances on their salespeople or had ignored the warning signs because the pressure to generate new revenue was so great.

At John Hancock, we worked hard to unravel this mess and made sure that it stopped. By the time the heavy-weight class-action lawyers began circling overhead and suing John Hancock and its competitors for astronomical sums, we were somewhat ahead of the game.

Nonetheless, there was a substantial cadre of lawyers, both Hancock lawyers and the company's outside lawyers, who wanted us to fight. It was all about minimizing the financial damage. Plus, there was a certain macho appeal to fighting, and litigators like to litigate.

I remember one meeting very distinctly: One guy was saying, "This lawsuit is going to drag out three to four years, and the burden of proof is going to fall on the customers, individual by individual. If we fight, we might be able to settle this down the road for just 20 or 30 cents on the dollar."

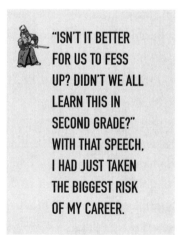

"ISN'T IT BETTER FOR US TO FESS UP? DIDN'T WE ALL LEARN THIS IN SECOND GRADE?" WITH THAT SPEECH, I HAD JUST TAKEN THE BIGGEST RISK OF MY CAREER.

Here was my response: "You are crazy. First of all, we did this. Second, our business stands for, 'When you die, we take care of your loved ones.' It does not stand for, 'When you die after having paid us three times more than you were supposed to, we take care of your loved ones.' Even if we could settle the class-action suit for 30 cents on a dollar, how much damage would our brand take, and how much would sales drop in the future? Isn't it better for us to fess up? Didn't we all learn this in second grade?"

With that speech, I had just taken the biggest risk of my career. And made many, many people unhappy.

I was inviting umpteen regulators to take a look at us, since we were regulated state by state, and assuring that we would have a lot of contact with class-action lawyers. Listening to blistering inquiries from both groups proved to be extraordinarily unpleasant.

It was also going to cost us some untold amount of money to make things right, hundreds of millions of dollars. First, we had to pay for an enormously expensive system to figure out fair compensation, customer by customer. Then, not only did we have to rebate the premiums that our customers had paid on "vanishing premium" policies, but we also had to give everybody the products we had promised at the price they thought they were buying them at, which was often at a steep loss for us. Not to mention the fact that we had already paid out millions to salespeople in commissions on these policies, many of whom were now gone with the wind.

THESE ARE NOT THE KINDS OF PRESSURES YOU FACE LOWER IN AN ORGANIZATION WHEN YOU'RE WORKING FOR ONE PERSON AND YOUR BIGGEST CHALLENGE IS GETTING A SINGLE PROJECT DONE ON TIME.

I made sure that some others were to follow. And none of this made me particularly popular with the remaining salespeople.

Because of my decision to admit our wrongdoing, we also did not know whether or not the company or individuals within it would be open to criminal prosecution.

In short, with this decision, I was volunteering everybody at John Hancock for a long, long period of humiliation—not to mention lower compensation as the company took the financial hit.

Remarkably enough, the CEO and the board supported me. So did a few of my colleagues. Aside from them, the only people pleased with my decision were the division heads in other parts of the company, who were buying drinks for each other, delighted to see a competitor in such an uncomfortable spot.

These are not the kinds of pressures you face lower in an organization when you're working for one person and your biggest challenge is getting a single project done on time. And nothing you've learned earlier in your career can prepare you for it.

You naturally start to doubt yourself in a situation like this. I wondered, "Am I overreacting? Being too moralistic, a goody two-shoes? If we could settle for 30 cents on the dollar, wouldn't that be better?" However, it had not been solely a moral decision. It also was a question of costs and benefits: Ultimately, what would hurt us the most?

And it was clear to me that we actually could have put the entire enterprise at risk by fighting, because we would have eventually lost. We then would have had to pay out far more money and would have been far more severely punished by our regulators. We would have hurt our brand, possibly permanently. And the whole process would have been paralytic to the company.

I credit my boss for recognizing the enterprise risk here and allowing me to make my decision. But no real reward followed it. Not once did anybody pat me on the back and say, "That was a really smart thing to do. We're glad you did it."

THE ONE RISK YOU MUST NEVER BE WRONG ABOUT IN YOUR CAREER IS ENTERPRISE RISK.

Then some of our competitors decided to fight rather than settle with the class-action lawyers, and they were lit up like Christmas trees.

Prudential, for example, seemed to be battling the inevitable every step of the way. Even after the company agreed to settle, some of the relevant sales documents were carelessly destroyed. There was a reluctance to share documents with customers who had decided not to participate in the class-action settlement. Even those customers who did participate accused the company of foot-dragging, stonewalling, and making the paperwork deliberately confusing.

The fight cost Prudential an astounding sum—according to court estimates, more than $3 billion by May 31, 2000. It also cost the company years of terrible newspaper headlines and a steep decline in the number of life insurance policies people bought from the company, which fell from about one million in 1991 to less than 300,000 in 1997. There was also considerable misery for the top executives there, including being forced to change their plans at Christmas after a judge ordered them to be deposed in the destruction of documents. While Prudential eventually righted itself, it was not before a lot of suffering.

> **EVERY PROJECT IN THE WORLD HAS A FATHER OR MOTHER WHO DECIDED TO TAKE THE RISK. AND ORGANIZATIONAL MEMORY IS VERY SHARP ON THIS POINT—WHO DECIDED TO TAKE THE RISK.**

The one risk you must never be wrong about in your career is enterprise risk. It doesn't appear that often, but there are times when, even in a position below CEO, you can actually put the entire organization in jeopardy. Just ask Andy Fastow, former CFO of Enron, or David Duncan, the partner in charge of the Enron account at the now-defunct accounting firm Arthur Andersen.

The problem with living in the vertical village of an organization is that you can become very provincial. Within that bubble, it's easy to forget how the outside world might view your actions and the degree to which your organization could be made to pay for them.

Enterprise risk, by the way, doesn't always take the form of scandal. I recently hired two companies, an air-conditioning company and a plumbing company, for a renovation. The owners worked on many of the same job sites and were in the process of merging.

Now, one would think that such a merger would be relatively easy. Two families, 20 employees each, pipes and water in common. But it is just as hard as a big merger. Questions such as "Who brought the newer trucks into the marriage?" and "Who is going to pay for the new trucks going forward?" are just as fraught with peril as any question in the AOL-Time Warner union.

This little merger also represents an enterprise risk. The two owners are making a potentially business-ending bet that, first, they will get along and, second, they will make more money because they have joined forces.

Even smaller risks are career makers or breakers. Every project in the world has a father or mother who decided to take the risk. And organizational memory is very sharp on this point—who decided to take the risk.

So you must learn to take risks in a calculated way. The worst sin is not to be able to understand the risks you face, either because you are so risk-averse that you say "No" to everything or because you have no risk filter whatsoever.

For example, I once had a senior executive who thought we ought to throw every conceivable product into the marketplace as quickly as possible, to the point where we had way too many products, many of which didn't function properly or were mispriced. Our salespeople, sensibly enough, were picking through this grab bag and only selling the ones that were well priced. But not necessarily for our profit. Well priced for their commissions. Needless to say, this executive soon lost all credibility with me on the product-development front.

> THE WORST SIN IS NOT TO BE ABLE TO UNDERSTAND THE RISKS YOU FACE, EITHER BECAUSE YOU ARE SO RISK-AVERSE THAT YOU SAY "NO" TO EVERYTHING OR BECAUSE YOU HAVE NO RISK FILTER WHATSOEVER.

Many people never rise above a certain level because they never see the downside of anything, particularly since it is not their own money at risk. This is a particular danger for people who start out in sales. They have to have such a positive attitude that they often lack any kind of risk DNA. They've knocked on a thousand doors and are used to getting a "No" before they get a "Yes." Therefore, everything to them is just a question of finding someone to say "Yes." The problem is that you're squandering your organization's resources on those yeses, and soon no one values your opinion.

Other managers become reckless in their risk taking simply because the pressure is on them to generate new revenue. I've seen university development people, for example, launch capital campaigns prematurely, before lining up big donors. They do it because their competition's doing it, and they fail miserably because they just haven't done the proper research.

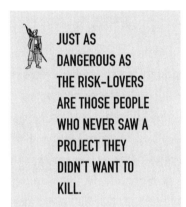

JUST AS DANGEROUS AS THE RISK-LOVERS ARE THOSE PEOPLE WHO NEVER SAW A PROJECT THEY DIDN'T WANT TO KILL.

Just as dangerous as the risk-lovers are those people who never saw a project they didn't want to kill. Everything's bad. Every potential product is bad, every proposal for a new computer system is bad, every new idea is bad.

These people often come from the financial side, where they have gotten the impression that things don't need to be sold in order for money to arrive. They're terrible for an organization because nothing ever gets done in their area. Their thinking is that if the risk is not taken, there is no downside.

Well, they're wrong. The downside is that no money comes in. Consider Detroit, where there seems to be a lot of these people. The mind-set is, "We've made big cars all of our lives. We're going to continue to make big cars. It's always served us well. If the public doesn't like it, too bad."

So then what happens is that the Japanese start making smaller, more fuel-efficient cars that are also more reliable, and Detroit gives up market share to Japan and begins a downward spiral. What's really unbelievable is that this same thing has now happened to the American car companies *twice* in my lifetime.

Playing safe is often the riskiest thing you can do in a career. If you stand still, the odds are overwhelming that the world will leave you behind.

BE OPEN TO NEW IDEAS, BUT DO THE WORK TO ANALYZE THE RISK.

You cannot encourage the people underneath you to play safe, either. You set the tone. If you have a low tolerance for any kind of mistake from the people who work for you, you will only get safe decisions from them.

The most successful organizations tend to be those where ideas flow freely, but where there are then mechanisms in place to analyze whether or not those ideas make sense. Try to follow the same pattern. Be open to new ideas, but do the work to analyze the risk. Surround yourself with people who can give you good answers as to what the risks really are.

Unfortunately, the more senior you become, the fewer mistakes you're allowed because bad outcomes become more public. If you bat .300, you're a star in Major League Baseball, even though you're wrong 70 percent of the time. Just try getting away with that in corporate life.

And if a risk goes south on you, you need to fess up early. I can remember when I first took over a big department at John Hancock, the Group

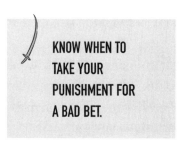

KNOW WHEN TO TAKE YOUR PUNISHMENT FOR A BAD BET.

Department. We were the largest group health and life insurer in the country. I had a bunch of IT people telling me that we had to put a new claims system in place.

Although it was going to cost $120 million, they promised that it would save us many millions every year. It seemed like a reasonable bet, except that the time frame kept moving outward and the price tag kept rising.

I was too young in my business career to understand what was really going on. There were hundreds of people working on this project, and they had gotten so deeply into it and were so delighted to be fully employed that they could no longer see the forest for the trees. The software they were developing was actually going to be obsolete by the time they finished. For all we were spending, we'd wind up behind our competitors.

GOOD LUCK OFTEN TAKES THE FORM OF HAVING THE RIGHT SKILLS AT THE RIGHT MOMENT.

One of the characters in my world finally saw that this was insanity, and she shared that insight with me.

For over a year, I had been extolling the virtues of this project to my bosses. Now I had to go to them and say, "Look, we're going to have to write off the $75 million we have into this. And we still don't have a system that works well because we have to go back to the old system."

I was chastised for letting the project go on longer than it should have, but I was also praised for not delaying any longer.

Know when to take your punishment for a bad bet. If I had waited another year and a half to take mine, it would have been worse. It would have been, "You, too, will be heading toward Siberia on a hay wagon."

LUCK: Smarter Than Reaching for the Brass Ring Is Letting It Slap You in the Nose

There is no such thing in this world as a pure meritocracy. Nobody gets to the top without being lucky. Luck happens to the most deserving of people and some of the most undeserving. It seems to me that George W. Bush got pretty lucky in 2000. It could just as easily have gone the other way.

When the *New York Times* asked Time Warner Chairman Richard Parsons in 2006 how he wound up running the company, he answered modestly, "Only in America. It's a society where a certain level of energy, grit, competence, and a huge dollop of luck enable somebody to go from the very bottom to the very top, or from the very top to the very bottom."

Good luck often takes the form of having the right skills at the right moment. Parsons, who is famously diplomatic, took over Time Warner at a moment when the Time Warner people were so bitter about their merger with AOL—and the subsequent decline in the value of their company stock—that civil war threatened. A diplomatic personality was just what was needed.

I certainly got lucky at John Hancock. The two CEOs before me were actuaries, and two of the finest executives I ever worked with. However,

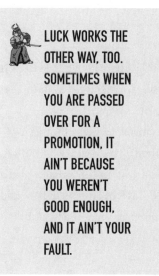

LUCK WORKS THE OTHER WAY, TOO. SOMETIMES WHEN YOU ARE PASSED OVER FOR A PROMOTION, IT AIN'T BECAUSE YOU WEREN'T GOOD ENOUGH, AND IT AIN'T YOUR FAULT.

you couldn't find a personality or background more different from the actuaries than mine. They were numbers people, I was a marketer. But Hancock needed top-line growth, and I was one of the few people inside who had demonstrated the ability to drive top-line growth.

Now, had I planned that there'd be two actuaries ahead of me? No. Had I planned that the company's biggest need in that era would be top-line growth? No.

And if the opposite had been true—that we had plenty of top-line growth but were having trouble making a profit on it—would I have been picked? Probably not.

Often you get the brass ring not because you reached so deftly for it, but because the brass ring smacked you in the nose. Little things can tip the balance. Somebody remembers a kindness that you paid them seven years ago or remembers something they read about you. And suddenly you're in.

Luck works the other way, too. Sometimes when you are passed over for a promotion, it ain't because you weren't good enough, and it ain't your fault. It happens in politics all the time. Very capable people are thrown out of office because their party is suddenly unfashionable. In 1994, the people of Washington State got rid of a sitting Speaker of the House, willing to sacrifice Tom Foley's clout to express their displeasure with the Democrats. The same kind of thing happens in universities and businesses, too. If the last head of the English Department was a Victorianist and fantastically unpopular, and you are a Victorianist, well, guess what? You are probably not going to be named department head.

So what can you do if you find yourself passed over for the promotion you should have gotten? Make your own luck.

TRY THE BEN FRANKLIN METHOD OF ADVANCEMENT:
Fly a Kite with Keys in a Rainstorm

If you are passed over for a promotion, think about trying a new instrument. Get assigned to task forces that cross divisions. Do whatever you can to be exposed to different disciplines. Contribute in new ways. Make sure you do all that you can to prove yourself, and then make it known that you're available to run a bigger show.

There are a lot of places, however, where you may never get the opportunity to test yourself outside your discipline because the discipline you want to move into already has so many good people.

When I worked for Commercial Credit, I knew there were armies of strong business managers already doing the kind of thing I wanted to do. Because it was an old mutual insurance company that had never had to fight for a stock price, John Hancock was not as rich in great managers. So when I got the chance to go to John Hancock, I leapt.

> IF YOU ARE PASSED OVER FOR A PROMOTION, THINK ABOUT TRYING A NEW INSTRUMENT.

Even if you are sure that you've found the right instrument, make sure that you are playing it in the right place. If your goal, for example, is to be a marketing chief, you would certainly want to be *from* Nike, one of the world's great marketing organizations, because you'd learn a tremendous amount there. But I'm not sure how long you would want to actually *be* there.

Nike has legions of fantastic marketing people. The competition for the top marketing spot is so intense there that your chances of getting the job are slim.

Remember also that by the time you get into your late 30s or so, you have another problem in an organization too rich in people with your skills: There is younger competition coming in underneath you. They are very, very smart. After all, they are Nike marketers. While you're waiting to move, they might move ahead of you.

 EVEN IF YOU ARE SURE THAT YOU'VE FOUND THE RIGHT INSTRUMENT, MAKE SURE THAT YOU ARE PLAYING IT IN THE RIGHT PLACE.

Stay too long at the Nikes of this world, and you may start to look like Rumpelstiltskin. You can spin straw into gold, but nobody knows your name.

So, at a certain point, go some place that really needs marketing talent. Go some place where the top people will brag about snagging you: "We have a guy who was in charge of the East Coast marketing for Nike, and he's now our national marketing manager."

That way, you can operate in a bigger landscape and get a chance to do what you always wanted to do.

Even for somebody at the level of Bob Nardelli, a change of venue can do wonders. He was ousted as CEO of Home Depot in 2007 in part because he couldn't get the stock to rise and in part because he was widely considered too impolitic for the head of a public company in today's world.

But then Chrysler was taken over by Cerberus Capital Management, a private equity firm. And the private equity world doesn't really care what public company analysts and business reporters think. Political finesse means nothing to them. They've got a Chrysler to rebuild and want a top-notch manager. So Bob Nardelli gets a second chance in an orchestra that is probably a better fit.

Not even the most powerful or ambitious person can force lightning to strike. But you can maneuver yourself into a position where it's more likely to strike. Figure out how to stand tall in an open field as soon as you can.

 STAY TOO LONG AT A PLACE TOO RICH IN YOUR SKILLS, AND YOU MAY START TO LOOK LIKE RUMPELSTILTSKIN. YOU CAN SPIN STRAW INTO GOLD, BUT NOBODY KNOWS YOUR NAME.

TWO

BOSSES

You Need a License to Cut Hair, but Not to Manage and Control Thousands of People

*If you think your teacher is tough,
wait till you get a boss.
He doesn't have tenure.*

Charles J. Sykes

While this book is about the many "bosses" you acquire as you rise, this particular chapter is about your relationship with that one person your organization calls your boss. Of course, if you happen to be unlucky enough to work for one of those matrix organizations where you not only report to the head of an individual business but also to the organization-wide grand pooh-bah boss in whatever your function happens to be . . . well, my condolences. You not only have many "bosses," you also have more than one actual boss to keep happy.

And that is difficult, because the relationship you have with your immediate boss is one of the oddest you'll have in life. You generally don't choose this person, you generally don't care for this person, yet you have to honor and obey this person. As you rise, that relationship only becomes odder and more slippery.

It's complicated now because you have some power of your own. You're no longer just a foot soldier. You may be running a legion of 5,000 soldiers, and your job is to protect that flank and take the Gauls over there. One minute you're barking orders at your troops, who look to you for direction. Then the next minute you have to ride the entire line and go to the general's tent. And now it's your turn to listen to orders.

You have to be very adroit at switching roles. At this level, I don't care whether your boss is a dictator, a deceiver, a maniac, or a pussycat. I can guarantee you one thing: That boss has a head somewhere between the size of a hotel room and an entire

> THE RELATIONSHIP YOU HAVE WITH YOUR IMMEDIATE BOSS IS ONE OF THE ODDEST YOU'LL HAVE IN LIFE. YOU GENERALLY DON'T CHOOSE THIS PERSON, YOU GENERALLY DON'T CARE FOR THIS PERSON, YET YOU HAVE TO HONOR AND OBEY THIS PERSON.

hotel. All day long people are telling your boss that she's right, and inevitably she starts to believe it. And at this level, it's a good bet that you have a head roughly half the size of a hotel room yourself and don't like being told what to do. Resentment on your part is natural.

GROW UP! YOUR BOSS IS NOT YOUR MOM OR DAD

You may try to camouflage that resentment by telling yourself that your relationship with your boss is like a relationship in a family, where you also don't always choose the people you report to. Actually, no. There is a very good chance that you are not going to go to the funeral of the person you spent 10 years with between the ages of 30 and 40. There's a good chance that if she outlives you, she won't come to yours. More than likely, there will be no lasting emotional tie.

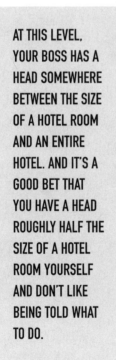

AT THIS LEVEL, YOUR BOSS HAS A HEAD SOMEWHERE BETWEEN THE SIZE OF A HOTEL ROOM AND AN ENTIRE HOTEL. AND IT'S A GOOD BET THAT YOU HAVE A HEAD ROUGHLY HALF THE SIZE OF A HOTEL ROOM YOURSELF AND DON'T LIKE BEING TOLD WHAT TO DO.

Early in your career, because you are so inexperienced and are generally working for people who are older than you, your relationship really does resemble that of student to teacher or parent to child. I say "resembles" for a reason. Real teachers, as we all know, are actually civic-minded. Real parents are actually self-sacrificing. In 35 years in organizational life, I have yet to meet the boss who is any such thing.

They may tell you, "I'm interested in making your career better."

But what they mean is, "I'm interested in making my *own* career better. If it happens to make your career better at the same time, then I'll claim credit for both. But I'm not going to be happy if your career gets better and mine doesn't."

Move toward the upper reaches of an organization, and even the pretense of parental concern tends to drop away. You are now an orphan. You cannot count on your boss to protect you now that you are visible to the president, the CEO, and the board. Mess up with these people, and you will be treated as roughly as Oliver Twist on the streets of London.

Your boss is not there to mentor you. At this level, she wants you for what you know, not for what she can nurture in you. And you are not there to serve her out of childlike gratitude, either.

The first rule of your relationship with your boss is to understand that it's a *business transaction*. That doesn't mean it has to be unpleasant. That doesn't mean some of your bosses won't be wonderful people. Some of mine were.

But it's a cold fact of ambition. If you really want to get to a place where there

THERE IS A VERY GOOD CHANCE THAT YOU ARE NOT GOING TO GO TO THE FUNERAL OF THE BOSS YOU SPENT 10 YEARS WITH BETWEEN THE AGES OF 30 AND 40. THERE'S A GOOD CHANCE THAT IF SHE OUTLIVES YOU, SHE WON'T COME TO YOURS.

are the fewest possible people issuing you orders—and the greatest number hanging on *your* every word—bosses are, at best, a means to an end. Most of the time, they are merely the major obstacle standing between you and the prize. Love them or hate them, what you really want is to get beyond them.

MAKE THINGS HAPPEN FOR THE BOSS

Though they come in all kinds of shapes and sizes, bosses are all interested in precisely the same thing—in having you make them look better. Anything else is incidental to them. So it's your job to make sure that you get something in return—that they help you rise.

To make the right deal with your boss, it's helpful to develop a healthy dose of cynicism about what the boss is up to.

No matter what bosses say, it's all about them. You are just an instrument to them. They'll treat you well as long as you're useful. On the other hand, I've never had a boss who hasn't expected 110 percent loyalty. No matter whether they were a former priest or perhaps headed in the other direction in the afterlife, they expected to be venerated.

THE FIRST RULE OF YOUR RELATIONSHIP WITH YOUR BOSS IS TO UNDERSTAND THAT IT'S A BUSINESS TRANSACTION.

And you have to put up with this imbalance because they have such enormous power over you, especially as you move up and start receiving complicated forms of compensation that vest over time. You become very much married to your boss, like it or not. So it's worth thinking about what it takes to be an effective instrument for the boss.

First of all, if your boss is any good, he is going to be searching for the truth.

The boss needs the truth to make good decisions. So you have to give him the truth, even when it's unpleasant.

I had a peer at John Hancock once who was so afraid to deliver bad news that he would try to disguise even the worst news as good news. Let's call him Tim. At one point, Tim's group lost a large commercial account that was not terribly profitable—but it was very important to the company in terms of prestige and helped us sell many other accounts.

Tim, however, went to the big bosses and said, "Well, we've lost it, but not to worry. It's not a big loss to the bottom line."

This was so transparently cowardly, I had to smile.

The boss is not stupid, so don't put a shine on the ball. At this level, you just don't. It frustrates the boss and makes you look like a lightweight.

If you *are* willing to give the boss the truth, you're probably going to engage in some spirited debate with your boss as part of the decision-making process.

This leads me to the second thing you need to do to be a valuable instrument: Understand that once the decision is made, even if you don't agree with it and have argued against it, you must drop your opposition and execute it to the best of your abilities.

Until you are in the top slot at your organization, you have exactly this much power: You have the right to carry out the boss's directive in the manner in which you believe it should be carried out. But you don't have the right not to carry out the directive or to alter its course dramatically. I can't tell you how many people I've seen actually confuse this.

NO MATTER WHAT BOSSES SAY, IT'S ALL ABOUT THEM. YOU ARE JUST AN INSTRUMENT TO THEM. THEY'LL TREAT YOU WELL AS LONG AS YOU'RE USEFUL.

For example, I had a guy who worked for me at John Hancock. When I would tell him, "I'm going to green-light these projects. Show me your timetable for delivering them," he would show me a timetable. And then he would go off and redo the timetable, as if we'd never talked about it, because he'd decided it was wrong.

What, are you kidding me?

You do, however, now have enough power not to put up with much nonsense. For example, I once had a boss who would schedule staff meetings and then bring his secretary in and dictate memos to *his* boss for an hour as we just sat there—and we were all senior people. The boss pretended that this was an efficient means of communicating with us, but it was really just raw arrogance. Excuse me, listening to dictation is not a staff meeting. So I just stopped going to the meetings.

It's okay to be a bad boy sometimes, if you do the third essential thing, which is help the boss move the ball from here to there.

Whether your boss is a bishop running a diocese who wants to build a new parish or the creative head of an advertising agency who wants to win a big new client, all bosses are trying to reach some goal. Make sure that you understand what your boss's goal is.

THE BOSS IS NOT STUPID, SO DON'T PUT A SHINE ON THE BALL.

It also is helpful to understand something beyond the immediate goal. I always wanted to know what my boss's next move was going to be. Did she want to keep rising within this company? Go someplace else? This is worth a conversation: "By the way, if we do these things successfully, where are you trying to go?"

If the boss said, "Look, I'm here just to help the organization do what's necessary," I always took that with an enormous grain of salt.

However, if you are working for a boss who is truly not ambitious—and hasn't yet set a nearby retirement date—that is a problem. This means that he is trying to play it safe. Playing it safe means you won't get noticed. Get behind a slow-moving train like this, and you are his caboose. There's a good chance you're going to get hit by a train behind you.

Bosses without ambition will reward the safe players over you, too. I mean, who plays it safe and surrounds himself with ambitious people? Nobody thinks, "You know what? I'm a giraffe. And I just want to mosey along here and eat from the trees. So what I'm going to do is herd a series of tigers and panthers to help me do that." Never happens.

A boss who has goals, a boss who will look you in the eye and tell you what those goals are and you can believe her—a boss like that is as good as gold.

The fourth thing you have to do is to assure the boss that you are both loyal and discreet. No matter how incompetent or unpleasant he may be, never tell stories about your boss. Never make the boss feel betrayed—unless, of course, you are ready to grab the boss's job, but we'll get to that in a minute.

Your goal here is to wind up as the most trusted person in the boss's stable. You want to be so trusted that you wind up as a de facto chief of staff. And you want to do that for one reason—because then you will get tremendous exposure to the most powerful people in your organization. Other people will come to you with messages for your boss. Your boss will send you out with messages for other people. This is the smartest possible way of building your own network and broadening yourself without being disloyal to your boss.

IF YOU ARE WORKING FOR A BOSS WHO IS TRULY NOT AMBITIOUS—AND HASN'T YET SET A NEARBY RETIREMENT DATE—THAT IS A PROBLEM.

The downside to becoming the favored implement in the boss's drawer is that she will become dependent on you. So it's your job to make a pact with your boss: "I'll help you reach your own goals, but you have got to do something for me, which is push me along."

If you fail to have a conversation like this with your boss, you are as dumb as mud. As I said before, it's all about them. It's a good bet that your boss does not spend much time thinking about you. So do not be lulled into assuming that she will help you move up just because she likes you. Don't assume that she will know or care where you want to go unless you tell her.

It's up to you to make sure that this relationship is a deal. Ask, "If we're successful here, what's going to happen to me?"

If the boss says, "Well, I can't tell you for sure," make sure that you talk about some options. And try to make sure that the promises are enforceable.

A CONTRACT BEATS A CARROT ANYTIME

The problem is that you often have to rely on the word of your boss, who may be utterly trustworthy or as manipulative as a snake. Let me tell you about the time I was wooed by the head of a good-sized advertising agency that employed 200 people. Let's call him Fred.

Fred played the part of the poor misunderstood entrepreneur and gave me this big song and dance: "The junior partners don't know what they're doing. I need someone smart like you."

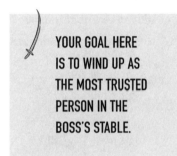

YOUR GOAL HERE IS TO WIND UP AS THE MOST TRUSTED PERSON IN THE BOSS'S STABLE.

He told me that I'd be the number two guy at the agency. He offered me more money than my father had made in 10 years, and I was only 30 years old.

I was ready to take the job after the first lunch. But Fred wanted to keep wooing, so we had lunch three times at the Four Seasons in New York City. Each time, he ruined more cloth napkins with his magic marker, sweetening my deal. He threw in a Corvette and a big advance and six weeks' vacation. And then for every account I landed, I would get 5 percent of the first year's billing.

Of course I took this deal. Wouldn't you? Coincidentally, Sparks Steak House was right across the street from my new place of employment, the spot where mafia boss Paul Castellano would be gunned down on John Gotti's orders. Something not entirely dissimilar happened to me.

Here I was, all enthusiastic, installed in an office next to the big boss—and Fred just threw me to the wolves. As soon as he got me there, he hardly deigned to say a word to me.

There was a new account we were pitching, and I stayed up two whole nights working on the presentation, which I was very proud of. I walked into Fred's office to show it to him and the first thing he said to me was, "Your hair is too long."

Then he flipped through the presentation, ripped it into four pieces, and threw it at my head, with a pleasant, "This is a pile of garbage. I can't be paying you all this money." And he walked out of his office and left the building.

That was the extent of my feedback. So what did I do? I went out and got a haircut.

Next, I went to tell one of the senior people this story and ask for some advice. He laughed. "Do you have the presentation on a word processor so you can make another copy?" he asked.

"Sure," I said.

"Use that."

"What do you mean?" I asked.

"Fred never looked at a word of it," the guy said sagely. "He's just teaching you who's boss."

The next time I saw Fred was at the client presentation. I used the same presentation he'd ripped up. The client gave us the account on the spot. Fred put his arm around me and told the client that I was the brand new star of the agency.

I was thinking to myself, "Why am I waiting for him to tell me my hair looks better?" Bosses can so mess with your psyche, if you let them.

At the end of the quarter, we got the first payment on this new account. I asked Fred about the 5 percent that was mine, and he said, "What percentage? I just made you that promise to get you here."

A lot of people live in places like that, where they are constantly being car-

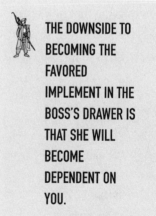

THE DOWNSIDE TO BECOMING THE FAVORED IMPLEMENT IN THE BOSS'S DRAWER IS THAT SHE WILL BECOME DEPENDENT ON YOU.

roted and sticked by manipulative bosses. It's not unusual for a boss to promise the same job to three people. And then the boss will come up with a series of excuses as to why you didn't get it.

People's hopes are often dashed because they depend on the word of people above them. In recent years, an awful lot of ambitious people have fallen asleep one night as an employee of a public company, only to wake up the next morning and find that they now work for private equity players. And in the aftermath of a merger or a leveraged buyout, the promises of even the most well-meaning bosses can be worthless.

Unless they are willing to put it in writing, don't believe it. So, whenever you can, get the promise in writing, and preferably on paper that comes out of a lawyer's laser printer rather than on a cloth napkin.

PROBLEM BOSSES ARE NOT RARE

One more Fred story: After I'd been with the advertising agency a few months, he threw a Christmas party for the office, spouses invited, at an artist's loft in Soho, a wonderful space. On the list of amenities was a hot tub. However, this was a formal party, suits and cocktail dresses with a lavish spread of food and drink, and nobody gave the tub a glance.

Within the first hour, our pasty, corpulent boss emerged from the back in a Speedo bathing suit, to the general astonishment. He mounted the wooden steps to the hot tub in Nero-like fashion and dropped himself into the tub, only to swear angrily. The tub was as cold as ice.

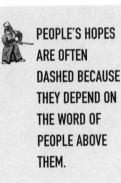

PEOPLE'S HOPES ARE OFTEN DASHED BECAUSE THEY DEPEND ON THE WORD OF PEOPLE ABOVE THEM.

Of course it was as cold as ice! The loft's owner didn't think it would be used for a formal Christmas party. Neither did any of us.

But Fred was beside himself with rage. One of his minions scurried for a giant towel, and as he was being wrapped up, he insisted that we all leave. So somebody found a big German restaurant that could take all of us, and the entire party moved. Three hundred people had to act as if nothing was wrong because we all needed to pretend we were working for someone sane.

I lasted just eight months before I realized that I had to go, not just because Fred was mad, but because he was making *me* insane. Anybody who assumes that the king knows what he's doing just because he's the king really needs to go buy the movie *The Madness of King George.*

Even when the king is not mad, he may well be incompetent. The Peter Principle, which says that people will rise to their level of incompetence, is quite flawed. It assumes that there's a ceiling, that once a boss reaches his level of incompetence, there are no further promotions.

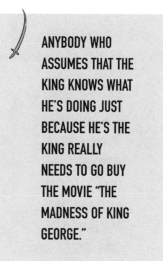

ANYBODY WHO ASSUMES THAT THE KING KNOWS WHAT HE'S DOING JUST BECAUSE HE'S THE KING REALLY NEEDS TO GO BUY THE MOVIE "THE MADNESS OF KING GEORGE."

I've seen thousands of people rise to their level of incompetence and continue to rise and be even more incompetent, in part because there are a lot of jobs that are just not measurable. If you are on the faculty of a university with a large endowment, and you are reasonably good at schmoozing the board and the kids, and are reasonably kind to your fellow professors, you can be there a very, very long time and even rise to provost or president while actually doing nothing to help the academic standing of the university.

I'm not recommending incompetence as a strategy for advancement. I'm just saying that people need a license to cut hair, but not to manage thousands of employees. So you can expect to run into incompetent bosses as you rise. And they may very well fail to fully appreciate how talented you are.

The good thing about even the worst bosses at this level is that while they can try to undermine you or compromise you, they cannot hide you.

GET INTO THE RIGHT MEETINGS, OR YOU MAY AS WELL STAY HOME

It's important to understand where the box of fairy dust is kept in your organization and make sure you are visible there. I know that when I was rising at the Hancock, there was never any question about who was in charge, and that was the CEO. Even though I had other bosses, some of whom were difficult, I worked very hard to make sure that I had a good relationship with the CEO.

Whoever the powers are in your organization, getting exposure to them is important. If your boss is carrying most of your work into meetings with the higher-ups but leaving you *out*, that's a problem. You just cannot allow it at this level. You have to say, "I want to present this." And if the boss does not agree, you have to either escape that boss or find another way in. If you have an ally who is invited to these meetings, ask her to say that she'd like your thoughts next time. Or ask her to get her boss to do it.

YOU CAN EXPECT TO RUN INTO INCOMPETENT BOSSES AS YOU RISE. AND THEY MAY FAIL TO FULLY APPRECIATE HOW TALENTED YOU ARE.

Chances are good that your boss won't even comprehend that he's been ambushed. He'll just say casually to you, "I've been thinking. You should be coming to these meetings."

Before you go to meetings with your boss and the top people in your organization, my advice is study, study, and study.

Why? Because until you are in one of the top slots, someone else in the room will be making the decisions. So you are there as a resource. And the most helpful thing you can offer is knowledge that allows the higher-ups to evaluate whatever issue is on the table.

Really knowing your stuff is what will get you invited back—and it's the only thing that will diminish your boss's control over you.

I guarantee that there are going to be questions in these meetings that your boss is not going to know the answers to. And if you study, you will. Your boss has a choice, really: "Do I turn to Sally here, or do I sound like a dunce? You know what I'll do? I'll take the credit for hiring a smart person."

Now the boss has to be a little more careful because the CEO has heard you offer something intelligent and will make up her own mind about you. If your boss criticizes you, a good CEO will now think, "I'll discount this because Joe here is trying to tamp Sally down."

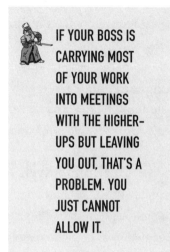

IF YOUR BOSS IS CARRYING MOST OF YOUR WORK INTO MEETINGS WITH THE HIGHER-UPS BUT LEAVING YOU OUT, THAT'S A PROBLEM. YOU JUST CANNOT ALLOW IT.

At some point, if you have impressed the CEO, she is going to initiate a conversation with you about your boss: "So how do you like working for Joe?"

You may find working for Joe about as enjoyable as having hives. But you'd better understand that answering a question like this is the organizational equivalent of crossing the open ocean in a one-person kayak.

The queen doesn't care how dangerous such a question is for you because she can't be harmed by the answer. But unless you have an exceptionally good relationship with the monarchy, you'd better assume that whatever you say will get back to the boss.

Being elusive and noncommittal and saying something vague like, "Working for Joe is fine," may seem like the smart strategy, but you risk insulting the CEO with your lack of trust in her discretion.

The safest course is to say something specific and complimentary: "Joe is really good at setting a direction for the group."

On the other hand, if you have a certain confidence in your relationship with the CEO, you might want to risk being more honest: "Joe is really good at setting a direction for the group, although he doesn't always explain it as well as he could." It's important that you be balanced and fair because chances are good, first, that the CEO placed Joe in his job and, second, that there is nothing negative you can say about Joe that she doesn't already know. Your manner may matter more than the content of your complaint.

So do not undermine Joe—if he hears about it, he will make you pay for it dearly—unless you have decided to try to dispose of him entirely. More about that in a minute.

HITCH YOUR CAREER TO AS MANY HORSES AS YOU CAN

If you help a boss achieve her ambitions—and she rises—you'll probably rise with her. But if I'd been able to predict with any accuracy in my own career who was going to rise, I would have quit business and made my living instead in Las Vegas.

I got my first hint that bosses can have surprisingly short life spans in the first grade. When you're about to go into first grade, all the older kids tell you scary stories about the teacher you're going to have. By the time I got there on the first day, though, and she showed me where the cloakroom was, I saw that she wasn't a monster, and all was well.

> **BEFORE YOU GO TO MEETINGS WITH YOUR BOSS AND THE TOP PEOPLE IN YOUR ORGANIZATION, MY ADVICE IS STUDY, STUDY, AND STUDY.**

Then, during our first art class, my teacher showed us how to use the paper cutter. She banged on the desks to emphasize that we should never, ever use the paper cutter alone. Over the summer, someone must have greased that paper cutter because it instantly fell and cut off her finger, which rolled off the desk onto the floor. So I was all set to have this teacher for the whole year, and in an instant, she was gone, and I had to get used to somebody new.

Your boss's future is just as uncertain.

When I worked at Control Data years ago, we had two major divisions. One sold computer time-shares that would allow companies that didn't want to invest in their own mainframe to use a satellite computer instead. This business was doing fantastically well, the most profitable business in the company.

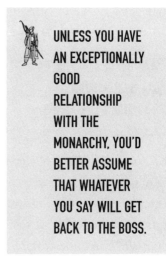 UNLESS YOU HAVE AN EXCEPTIONALLY GOOD RELATIONSHIP WITH THE MONARCHY, YOU'D BETTER ASSUME THAT WHATEVER YOU SAY WILL GET BACK TO THE BOSS.

The other division sold something less glamorous—data-processing services for payrolls and general accounting. This business was merely trundling along. A guy named Bob ran it. When we had our monthly staff meeting, Bob would come with his charts and show all his numbers. He was struggling, his expenses were high, but there was nothing arrogant about him. He just kept pushing the business along.

Running the time-sharing, on the other hand, was a guy named Mickey, an unpleasant guy with a Marine's haircut. He was really just riding a trend but was so arrogant that you'd think he'd built this success out of sheer genius. He'd come to the monthly staff meeting, and when his turn to present came around, he would just pull a little scrap of paper out of his pocket and drawl, "Yeah, sales were up 28 percent this month."

The president never said to him, "I want to see charts from you like I see from everybody else." He just waited. He waited until it was time for a change and the brass ring was on the table. Then he gave it to somebody else—to Bob, who was now Mickey's boss.

There were many astonished people in that organization, namely a whole army of fraternity types who'd tied their careers to Mickey because his numbers were so outstanding. They'd spent 10 years following him, becoming just as arrogant and difficult as he was, assuming that they'd rise when he did. They pissed away 10 years of their lives.

Me, I was always loyal to Bob because I liked his style and considered him the total manager. But my advice here is *not* to choose wisely when you're deciding which horse to hitch yourself to.

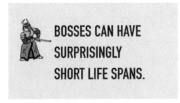

BOSSES CAN HAVE SURPRISINGLY SHORT LIFE SPANS.

My advice is: Don't hitch yourself just to the best manager. Don't hitch yourself just to the favorite. Don't hitch yourself just to your own boss. Instead, understand that your career chariot does not have just one set of reins—and hitch yourself to as many people as possible.

You cannot predict what will happen in organizational life. You can waste five years following somebody who decides one morning that he wants to take an early retirement. I guarantee that this guy is not saying to himself: "You know what? I'd really like to retire early, but I'm not going to because David is depending on me."

Another boss might decide, "I'm going to Lehman Brothers." She might make a deal with the bosses upstairs to get her bonus and have her options vested in return for one concession: She won't take anybody with her for two years. What if you've been counting on riding this boss's coattails? "So long, farewell, *auf Wiedersehen*, good night."

DON'T HITCH YOURSELF JUST TO YOUR OWN BOSS. INSTEAD, HITCH YOURSELF TO AS MANY PEOPLE AS POSSIBLE.

You simply cannot depend on any one individual to carry you. And if your reputation is that of one boss's Quasimodo, it's a good bet that any new boss is going to look at you as someone he doesn't want.

The trick is to ride a bunch of horses without running into conflict. And you can do this by being a good interpreter between camps. Carry information. Be a go-between—be discreet about it—and you'll win the loyalty of a lot of potential risers.

This is so important because if you are doing a good job for your boss, that boss may well try to hang onto you in your current position. Nobody gives up a top-notch person just because it's the right thing for the employee. I'll bet that doesn't even happen in the Vatican.

If you are top-notch, your boss will probably only give you up if you are otherwise going to leave the organization—or if she is ordered to, or if another power in your organization offers her an interesting deal for you.

So having that outside network may well be the key to your ascent.

BEWARE THE MENTOR

Unless your boss is very, very strong, he is likely to have moments of paranoia as you gain power and he suddenly feels your hot breath at the back of his neck.

Nothing is more frightening to most bosses than the idea that someone they have brought along might become their equal—or even surpass them and become their boss. "That's the guy who used to wait outside with a cup of coffee while I dictated to my secretary. He is now telling *me* what to do?" They know it means they are now obsolete.

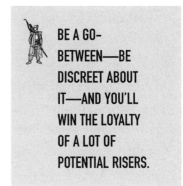

BE A GO-BETWEEN—BE DISCREET ABOUT IT—AND YOU'LL WIN THE LOYALTY OF A LOT OF POTENTIAL RISERS.

And that sense of jealousy and betrayal is most acute when they are emotionally invested in you. So beware the mentor. He brings you along, and in return, he expects lifelong fealty. "I found you. I gave you promotions. How could you possibly disagree with me? How could you possibly leave me? How could you possibly rise to my level and keep me awake nights with the fear that someday I might have to work for you?"

The mentor thinks that he is the hare and you're the tortoise. He may do wonderful things for you early in your career—protect you, teach you, encourage you. But if you catch up with him, it can get really ugly.

Before I worked at Hancock, I once had a boss with whom I was really close. We'll call him Carl. He was one of the few people in my career I'd consider a mentor, and he'd really brought me along. However, there had already been some chafing as I had risen in the organization and won favor with some of the top people. I was now in a position where I could express opinions Carl disagreed with, and to his frustration, he could no longer simply veto my ideas.

Then, one morning, my brother called to tell me about a crisis in our family, and it was clear that I had to travel home.

NOTHING IS MORE FRIGHTENING TO MOST BOSSES THAN THE IDEA THAT SOMEONE THEY HAVE BROUGHT ALONG MIGHT BECOME THEIR EQUAL.

Carl offered to fly out to lend a hand. While I really appreciated his concern, I explained to him that I was going to have my hands full with my crazy family. If I had to focus on friends from another environment as well, it would only make things more difficult for me.

I wasn't back in the office but a few hours when Carl handed me a letter accusing me of being ungracious and inconsiderate for not allowing him to come along.

In turn, I found him utterly inconsiderate. And unreasonable.

This evolved into a very ugly argument—such an ugly argument that, except when work demanded it, we never said a word to each other again.

Carl had actually been one of the very few men in my life I'd cared about as much as my father. But, when I'd made the distinction between boss and family clear, he'd been mortally offended.

Mentor relationships often end in such train wrecks. The famously close relationship between Sandy Weill, the former chairman of Citigroup, and his protégé, Jamie Dimon, offers another good example. From the time Dimon was 26, they'd worked side by side as Weill had built his empire. In a 2005 interview with the *New York Times*, Weill reflected on their bond and said he viewed Dimon "as close to a member of my family." But by the time Dimon reached his early 40s, things were growing tense.

In the autobiography he wrote with Judah S. Kraushaar, *The Real Deal: My Life in Business and Philanthropy*, Weill describes a classic power struggle between the generations:

> By 1997, Jamie had become fixated on the notion that I hadn't recognized his contributions. He also exuded a sense of empowerment . . . and increasingly challenged me to the point of rudeness in front of other executives. . . . In a surprisingly short time, I felt Jamie had changed from being a loyal lieutenant to running a company within a company, and I began to wonder if he ultimately sought to push me aside altogether.

Then an actual family member—Weill's daughter Jessica Bibliowicz—left Citigroup, where she had run Smith Barney's mutual fund business, because Dimon wasn't promoting her quickly enough. "Jamie's lack of follow-up infuriated me—Jessica might have ended up staying if only Jamie had demonstrated his support for her," Weill writes. By 1998, this father-son-like relationship was over. Dimon was fired.

MENTOR RELATIONSHIPS OFTEN END IN TRAIN WRECKS.

If you want unconditional love, turn to your family, because you won't get it from a boss—or a protégé. Whenever a boss said to me, "You're like a son to me" or "You're like a brother to me," it scared me. I'd feel like Fredo being embraced by Al Pacino in *The Godfather, Part II*. I was afraid I was going to be taken out in a boat.

Of course, both Dimon and Bibliowicz went on to be extremely successful: Dimon become CEO of JPMorgan Chase, and Bibliowicz, CEO of National Financial Partners.

Don't be surprised if you, too, have to leave the nest to really soar.

SEIZE THE CHAIR

The most dangerous place you can be in organizational life is the same as the most dangerous place in marital life—at one point of a triangle. In this case, the other two points include somebody at the top of your organization who likes you—and a boss who possibly feels betrayed by you.

If your boss fears you are moving up on him, he may well decide to diminish your role or do you in. In such a case, you must act quickly. Chances are, since he has greater access to the board and the CEO, he can do more damage to you over a long period of time than you can do to him. And if you let him go on undermining you too long, at most places the best that can happen is that he does both of you in.

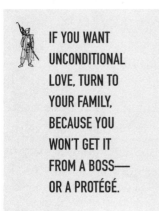

IF YOU WANT UNCONDITIONAL LOVE, TURN TO YOUR FAMILY, BECAUSE YOU WON'T GET IT FROM A BOSS—OR A PROTÉGÉ.

That is why it is important to get a really, really strong sense of where your boss stands with the top decision makers in your organization. Gossip is worthless in such a situation. I never listened to someone who told me, "Oh, the CEO's unhappy with so and so," because I couldn't be sure what stage the rumor was in, whether it was first-hand information or fourth-hand.

Instead, pay sharp attention in the meetings you attend. Watch the body language particularly carefully. What do the board and the other senior people do when your boss presents? If the CEO is rolling her eyes or looking the other way or doodling while your boss is talking, you'll get an idea. You will then know how much room you have to maneuver out from under your boss.

And if you can't tell how good the relationship is between your boss and the top decision maker? I suggest you find another way to make a living.

If your boss has a strong relationship with the CEO and is trying to do you in, chances are good that you are toast. But chances are also good that if your boss had a strong relationship at the top of the house, he wouldn't be trying to do you in. He's only trying to do you in because he's insecure.

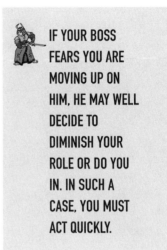 IF YOUR BOSS FEARS YOU ARE MOVING UP ON HIM, HE MAY WELL DECIDE TO DIMINISH YOUR ROLE OR DO YOU IN. IN SUCH A CASE, YOU MUST ACT QUICKLY.

That's when you take your chance. Before too much water goes under your bow, go to somebody senior and say, "I really like working here, but I can't work with Joe anymore. He's too difficult. He's not letting me bring my own ideas forward. I don't want to appear to be disloyal to him, but I want to work someplace else."

Or if you sense that your boss is really weak, you might even do what somebody I know once did. Go to the CEO and say, "My boss is sitting in my chair." And make your case for why Joe's job should be yours.

PAY SHARP ATTENTION IN THE MEETINGS YOU ATTEND. WATCH THE BODY LANGUAGE PARTICULARLY CAREFULLY.

Of course, to do this, you have to be either very confident or so fed up that anything is better than the status quo. You'd better have an exit plan, too, either in the form of another job offer or sufficient savings to get by.

You'll have to give the top decision maker time to think about it. But sometimes the sheer audacity of the move will impress the CEO, and you'll not only escape a problem boss, you'll get his office and comfortable couch, too.

THREE

3

PEERS

Understand That They Are Your Most Valuable
Allies . . . or Your Most Dangerous Enemies

*Never interrupt your enemy when
he is making a mistake.*

Napoleon Bonaparte

If you are an ambitious person, one of the most convenient ways for a boss to find fault with you is to decide that you are not a "team player." This charge is commonly used in organizational life in part because it's so hard to defend yourself against it. What are you going to say? "Yes, I do love my fellow man" is hardly convincing. And such an accusation will invariably provoke a head-shaking "tsk-tsk" reaction in any powerful person who hears such a thing about you. Never fails!

The incestuous logic is that only team players can be trusted to put the organization's interests before their own, so only team players can be trusted with the big jobs. As a result, if you appear to be openly aggressive or uncooperative with your peers, it can put the brakes on your career.

But let's admit, most ambitious people are not naturally team players. They're ruthlessly competitive individualists. They've been challenging their peers since they were three years old, trying to be the one who swings highest at the playground. In school, in sports, in the office, that's what has gotten them where they are, and they see no reason to stop.

MOST AMBITIOUS PEOPLE ARE NOT NATURALLY TEAM PLAYERS. THEY'RE RUTHLESSLY COMPETITIVE INDIVIDUALISTS.

I've never witnessed a clearer demonstration of most up-and-comers' attitudes toward their peers than when I was at Citibank in the early 1980s, on a retreat in the Catskills, of all places—the Borscht Belt, comedy capital for summering New Yorkers in the 1940s and 1950s, the aging resort where people like Jackie Mason and Rodney Dangerfield had made their names. It didn't seem to be a particularly appropriate choice for Citibank, except that those of us attending the retreat didn't get no respect, either.

One of the things that happens to you in any kind of organization as you rise is that your bosses increasingly see the value of training you, so they are more and more likely to send you to an off-site to learn something. Some of these are worthwhile, namely, the highly technical courses that teach you a particular skill. On the other hand, few things are worse in a career than being sent to one of those Outward Bound off-sites to learn "leadership" while wearing damp hiking boots and swatting off mosquitoes.

There is an entire multi-billion-dollar industry designed to teach people skills such as team-building, and you will never meet more arrogant men and women in your life than these people experts because they unfailingly treat everybody like third graders.

 FEW THINGS ARE WORSE IN A CAREER THAN BEING SENT TO ONE OF THOSE OUTWARD BOUND OFF-SITES TO LEARN "LEADERSHIP" WHILE WEARING DAMP HIKING BOOTS AND SWATTING OFF MOSQUITOES.

On this particular retreat, Citibank brought in some instructors with Harvard credentials and put us all up in a series of log cabins for a course about managing people. A harmless enough venture on the surface, but Citibank at that time was a very, very competitive place. Truly a place of the best and brightest, lots of stars. People who, for the most part, behaved like piranhas because they were hunting all the time—hunting for funding, hunting for projects, hunting for ways to beat up the other divisions and make more money than they did.

Nonetheless, the theory was that after two weeks of dirt roads and pine needles and no alcohol, we'd all come out as "people" people. There were about 20 of us in the class, mostly midlevel managers who were relatively new to the company and strangers to each other, plus a few more powerful types who were in the dog house. If you go to one of these things and there is a senior vice president among you, you know that he or she has committed some political blunder and is there to be "sensitized." It's the corporate equivalent of being sent to a Maoist reeducation camp.

At the end of the first night, the instructors did this exercise that I had never seen before, which is quite common now, where you pick a partner, who blindfolds you, and then you allow yourself to fall backward into your partner's arms. As I fell, one of the instructors was telling us, "It's all about building trust. . . . "

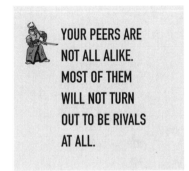

YOUR PEERS ARE NOT ALL ALIKE. MOST OF THEM WILL NOT TURN OUT TO BE RIVALS AT ALL.

When my head hit the floor, three things made me feel better. One, I heard a lot of other heads hit the floor, too. Two, we were on a plush carpet, so it wasn't too painful. And three, the guy laughing behind me, the guy who'd let me fall—well, it was his turn to wear the blindfold next. Oops!

So there we were, the best and the brightest, future leaders and exemplars, all behaving like the jealous teenagers in the Lindsay Lohan movie *Mean Girls*.

I do not suggest that you treat your peers this way. It's stupid for many reasons, including the fact that your peers are not all alike. Most of them will not turn out to be rivals at all. For every peer who is truly running against you for the next job, there are probably five who are not even in the race.

They may be less ambitious than you, satisfied with where they are. Or they may be in staff positions—in the general counsel's office, in finance, in public relations, in information technology, or in human resources. These peers may rise to the top of their area of expertise, but they probably won't wind up running the organization. As a general rule, if you are not in a revenue- or profit-generating position, you don't get the top spot.

Or they may simply have the wrong talents or the wrong temperament for leadership. The real rivals among your peers will be room-changers. Certain people, when they walk into a room, alter the atmosphere. Everybody else adjusts their posture, their willingness to listen, their ideas. This is not a full definition of leadership, only its most obvious symptom.

Presumably you are a room-changer—and so is every one of your real opponents. If they are smart, your peers who are *not* room-changers already understand that they will probably end up working for one of you.

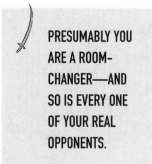

PRESUMABLY YOU ARE A ROOM-CHANGER—AND SO IS EVERY ONE OF YOUR REAL OPPONENTS.

Keep this in mind, however. Just because your peers in the spectator seats are not there in the ring with you and the other gladiators battling for the next big promotion, that does not mean they are passive or docile. Instead, they are going to work very hard to play the Nero role here—thumbs up or thumbs down—and will try to influence the outcome of the contest in a way favorable to themselves.

As a result, they can be the most valuable of allies . . . or the most dangerous of enemies.

CULTIVATING THE "CONSIGLIERI" (ALSO KNOWN AS SUCKING UP)

Here is the source of the also-rans' power: They are often trusted by the boss in a way that you and the real contenders are not.

If you're a contender, the boss knows your ambitions, knows that you're willing to take risks to promote yourself, and suspects that you might lead her into recklessness. Most top executives are risk-averse. They've already gotten to the top. They don't need to take as much risk. They'll take some risk for the sake of the company, certainly, but they won't take a lot of unnecessary personal risk.

The people who are not in line for big promotions, on the other hand, are seen by the bosses as disinterested and therefore saner judges of what's best for the organization. As a result, they often become *consiglieri*, or the real advisors behind the throne. This is particularly true for intelligent people in staff positions in human resources, public relations, investor relations, or the law department.

You can identify the *consiglieri* by their unfettered access to the boss. These are the people able to walk into the office of the executive director or president or CEO on a moment's notice and just glide past the assistant, with or without an appointment.

You need to be aware of who gets to see the big boss alone for an hour a week and, unless you are particularly self-destructive, try not to alienate them. People talk, and it is certain that at some point the big boss will ask the *consiglieri* what they think of you. The damage they can do in three minutes is considerable: They can do you in before coffee is served.

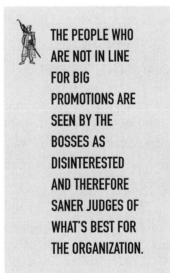

THE PEOPLE WHO ARE NOT IN LINE FOR BIG PROMOTIONS ARE SEEN BY THE BOSSES AS DISINTERESTED AND THEREFORE SANER JUDGES OF WHAT'S BEST FOR THE ORGANIZATION.

Sometimes, you won't be able to help making an enemy of a *consigliere*. But do go out of your way *not* to tick off the head of human resources or the general counsel. Nothing is more terrifying to the top management of any organization than the prospect of scandal. So nothing scares them off a person more than a negative opinion on the part of the head lawyer or the human resources chief.

All the general counsel has to say is, "I'm not sure about that woman's ethics. I think she might get you in trouble," and your career can sustain terrible damage.

Once, in New York, I had a poor relationship with the head of personnel for the division I was working in, a woman we'll call Carol. And it cost me dearly with my boss at the time. When I had to fire somebody,

I always did the best I could. But Carol would make sure that the president of the division, who listened to her, heard that I was needlessly cruel.

He'd ask me, "How'd it go with Mike's firing?"

I'd answer, "It went fine," initially having no idea that the dark mat had been laid at my feet.

"Well, that's not the way I hear it," the president would say. "I heard Mike came out crying."

"It wasn't easy," I'd say, "but I don't remember any tears."

And in his eyes, because Carol had fed him this negativity, I was either insensitive or lying. It was a lose-lose situation for me.

 IT IS CERTAIN THAT AT SOME POINT THE BIG BOSS WILL ASK THE "CONSIGLIERI" WHAT THEY THINK OF YOU. THEY CAN DO YOU IN BEFORE COFFEE IS SERVED.

Finally, after a series of these body blows, I'd had enough. The next time my boss called me on the carpet for some personnel matter, I said, "Ah, don't tell me, let me guess. Carol has been in your office lately. Do you see a pattern here?"

"Well," he said, "do you and Carol not get along?"

"I don't think we do, but that's all I'm going to say. If you would like to know how my next firing goes, why don't you ask the person who gets fired? There are two people in the room, not three."

That worked because I was able to point out that Carol was *not* disinterested—she had it in for me. And I managed to diminish her trustworthiness as an advisor.

LET THE CONSIGLIERI HELP YOU ACCOMPLISH GREAT THINGS

Cultivating the *consiglieri* is not just a smart defensive move. They can also be extraordinarily helpful as you struggle to get things done.

You have to realize that whenever you propose a new fund-raising idea, a new curriculum for the undergraduates, a new product, or a new acquisition, your boss is looking at you through narrowed eyes thinking, "I need your drive, but I wonder if your ambition isn't making you irresponsible."

So I almost never introduced my big ideas to the boss myself. Instead, I would take one of the *consiglieri* aside and consult him.

"Look, I have this product idea," I might say. "What do you think?" And if he approved, I'd then say, "Well, if you happen to meet with the boss in the next week or so, would you mind mentioning it to him?"

The *consigliere* is soon sitting with the boss and saying, "You know, the people in the retail division are thinking about something new, and it looks like a pretty good product."

Get one of your peers to break the ice for you this way, and you'll find that when you walk into the boss's office three weeks later to make your pitch, you are far more likely to get a positive reception—first, because the boss has heard the idea from someone he trusts, someone who has no business agenda, and second, because the boss is pleased with himself for being so ahead of the game.

Use your peers in this way and they can have a lot of influence on your success. Let's make no mistake about it, you are using them. They are carrying your water on important decisions. But it's also good for them because it allows them to demonstrate to the boss how ahead of the curve *they* are. Classic washing of each other's hands.

> GET ONE OF YOUR PEERS TO BREAK THE ICE FOR YOU, AND YOU'LL FIND THAT WHEN YOU WALK INTO THE BOSS'S OFFICE TO MAKE YOUR PITCH, YOU ARE FAR MORE LIKELY TO GET A POSITIVE RECEPTION.

The key thing to understand is that such a relationship only works if you are willing to be generous with the credit for your great idea—and not just at the awards dinner, either.

I always find it false when someone publicly announces at the end of a project, "Well, it never would have been possible without Glenn, Sarah, and Terry," after the speaker has taken credit for every single aspect of the project for months. The truly sophisticated player allows others to contribute and gives them public credit along the way, during the real working meetings.

 IT'S NOT IMPORTANT TO BE THE SOLITARY GENIUS WHO DREAMED UP, FINANCED, AND IMPLEMENTED A GREAT PLAN ALL BY YOURSELF. WHAT'S REALLY VALUABLE IS SHOWING THAT YOU ARE THE KIND OF PERSON OTHER POWERFUL PEOPLE WANT TO WORK WITH.

In return, you'll have to sacrifice being the carrier of all the positive messages. But the truth is that it's not important to be the solitary genius who dreamed up, financed, and implemented a great plan all by yourself—or even desirable. What's really valuable is showing over and over that you are the kind of person other powerful people want to work with.

Of course, there's a corollary to sharing success: You have to be equally generous when things go wrong. *Never* ask one of your peers to carry bad news for you. If there's going to be a disaster in any part of the organization that you're running, whether it's a personnel issue or a financial issue, always inform the boss yourself. Make an arrangement with your boss. Figure out how late you can call her at night, and then make sure that she hears about anything negative from your lips.

If, God forbid, you allow an enemy to deliver bad news before you do, you are compounding the strikes against you. First, it looks as if you are hiding this news. Second, your enemy gets credit for being a "team player," and you don't. So your choice is castor oil—or a rocket fuel enema. Ouch!

I suggest that you pick the lesser of two evils and swallow the castor oil. Not only will your boss respect your courage, but your staff peers will realize that you're willing to take responsibility for your own problems. This builds a trust you cannot build in another way.

I can remember a quarter at John Hancock when there was going to be a $15 million loss in my area that no one had expected. I asked the financial office not to tell the CEO and the president because I wanted to tell them myself. The financial people were pretty surprised at that because they are often the bearers of bad news. But they respected me for it and, as a result, kept me highly informed about what was going on in the organization.

This is important because, as far as I'm concerned, the most valuable weapon you can have in any contest for the top is information. If I was going into a general management meeting

NEVER ASK ONE OF YOUR PEERS TO CARRY BAD NEWS FOR YOU.

and a rival was going to be there, I wanted to know as much as she did about whatever she was going to talk about. Because I had created allies among my peers, I generally got that information.

You need eyes and ears wherever you can win them, not to learn the latest gossip, but to cross lines in terms of the business and find out what you are otherwise not in a position to know. Your bosses are going to promote the person who is best able to grasp the organization as a whole, so reach across borders whenever you can.

Get to know the people at your level in all parts of your organization. Not only will they give you insights into what's happening in the organization at large, they may even be key to your longevity.

DON'T CONFUSE YOUR BOSS'S ENEMIES WITH YOUR OWN

One of the most dangerous situations you can find yourself in is one in which your boss is battling with a handful of his peers for control of an organization. If you are too tightly aligned with that boss, and he loses, all bets are off on your career, too.

Let me tell you about my own experience as a spear carrier in such a fight to the finish. During the early 1980s, I worked for Commercial Credit, a subsidiary of Control Data, which was once a great computer company that had rivaled IBM—but had since bought dozens, if not hundreds, of unrelated businesses. It had turned into one of those Noah's Ark corporations, where everything belonged simply because it was in the animal kingdom.

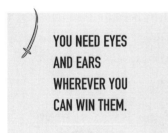

YOU NEED EYES AND EARS WHEREVER YOU CAN WIN THEM.

At the Control Data headquarters in Minneapolis, somebody had the idea of using a lot of these mismatched beasts in a new type of business center, a pre-Kinkos kind of place where you could improve your mind using PLATO, Control Data's interactive educational system. Or you could use a Control Data mainframe to get your payroll processed. Or you could buy business insurance. Or you could get a loan for your business. Or you could buy a building to house it.

It was one-stop shopping, as convenient and appealing as being able to go to a tire store to buy cologne.

At first, Control Data had four or five different divisions in various parts of the country creating these business centers, and the race was on as to whose concept was the smartest. Then, after many, many millions of dollars had been wasted, instead of abandoning this flawed idea, headquarters decided to consolidate all these competing efforts in Baltimore under Commercial Credit, a consumer finance company, the very least likely place to put it. That way we could waste even more money—in one location instead of five.

So dozens of executives were transferred to Baltimore from all over the country and began to form new teams. Some were legitimate executives taking their best people with them. And some were the worst people being off-loaded by the corporation like Castro emptying out the jails in Cuba and sending five boats an hour to Miami. And, of course, no such folly would be complete without a handful of corporate spies.

Adding interest to this already interesting mix were the higher-ups from the existing consumer finance business in Baltimore, many of whom got their start going door-to-door collecting deadbeat loan payments for cars and refrigerators. Now they were executives, but some of them never did rid themselves of the habit of carrying a gun from their days as debt collectors. Trust me, there is nothing like sitting in a meeting with a dinosaur of an executive and noticing the handle of a .38 caliber peeking out from under his belt. Alarming does not begin to describe the experience.

And just to complicate things even more, in the middle of this race, we acquired ERA, the big real estate company. What did we know about real estate? Nothing, except that we had an Ark, and therefore it belonged on the Ark.

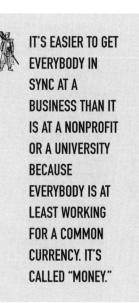

IT'S EASIER TO GET EVERYBODY IN SYNC AT A BUSINESS THAN IT IS AT A NONPROFIT OR A UNIVERSITY BECAUSE EVERYBODY IS AT LEAST WORKING FOR A COMMON CURRENCY. IT'S CALLED "MONEY."

Add it all up, and Commercial Credit was a very strange and dangerous place. What had been a contest between one or two Commercial Credit executives for the president's office was now a race among six people who barely knew each other. Everybody was divided into warring camps, complete with all the territorial jealousies, deceit, corporate politics, and naked aggression one might expect.

But we were supposed to play nice. We were creating one-stop-shopping centers that would pluck products from all our different businesses, so all the staffers had to at least appear to work together. Not a chance!

Ideally, in any organization, you're all sitting in the same boat, and you're all rowing together. And the truth is that it's easier to get everybody in sync at a business than it is at a nonprofit or a university because everybody is at least working for a common currency. It's called *money*. In a corporation, you can actually dislike each other quite a bit, and it may not be pretty, but you will still make sausage. "We're not making sausage" discussions are not allowed.

Unless, of course, you happen to be in the middle of a race like this, where your primary concern is your own survival. And in the short run, that survival depends not on the whole organization doing well but only on your boss getting promoted and carrying you with him. Needless to say, this is not a very brilliant way to run a railroad, but that's a different issue. The question is, if you find yourself in a situation like this, what do you do?

 HE WAS A STRATEGIC PLANNER, WHICH IN CORPORATE LIFE IS A EUPHEMISM FOR EITHER "A VERY SMART PERSON I DON'T KNOW WHAT TO DO WITH" OR "SOME BOSS'S COUSIN."

I remember one guy who worked for the head of the retail divisions of Commercial Credit. Let's call him Steve. He was a strategic planner, which in corporate life is a euphemism for either "a very smart person I don't know what to do with" or "some boss's cousin."

Steve was neither as smart nor as connected as he should have been, but he was plenty arrogant. He decided on a very aggressive approach with his peers in the other divisions, lobbying us constantly for his boss, trying to push his boss's products through, attempting to argue us into cooperating with him.

As a result, we wouldn't do a thing for him. The corporate cold shoulder. It was amusing because we would be in very serious meetings, and Steve would be there strenuously defending his boss's point of view and be completely ignored. His boss was weak and could do nothing about it, either, except whine and blather.

What was Steve's reward for loyalty? Why, his boss cut him loose before the race was even decided. As Donald Trump would say, "You're fired!" He'd become a liability. Off the Ark and into the water.

Tensions inevitably run high in a horserace like this. In *Jack: Straight From the Gut*, the autobiography Jack Welch wrote with John A. Byrne, Welch describes the politics surrounding his own contest for the chairmanship of General Electric as "thick." He recounts the experience of one executive underneath him who backed a rival: "Paolo Fresco, then a vice president, recalls being nearly physically confronted in a Fairfield hallway by an overzealous executive who reported to Burlingame yet supported me. Fresco remembers being called a 'jackass' simply because he was loyal to his own boss."

Fresco did indeed make a less-than-perceptive choice, and when Welch won, proffered his resignation. Welch refused to accept it, and Fresco went on to become one of his most trusted executives. But then Welch was a legendarily great recognizer of talent. You cannot count on any such forgiving genius winning control of your organization. And if you are the person roughing up your peers in the hall—and your boss turns out not to be the Jack Welch of the group—brace yourself.

The fact is, making enemies of your peers out of excessive loyalty to your boss in a situation like this is the equivalent of buying your own six-chamber revolver and playing Russian roulette—only with the propor-

> **MAKING ENEMIES OF YOUR PEERS OUT OF EXCESSIVE LOYALTY TO YOUR BOSS IS THE EQUIVALENT OF BUYING YOUR OWN SIX-CHAMBER REVOLVER AND PLAYING RUSSIAN ROULETTE—ONLY WITH THE PROPORTIONS REVERSED: FIVE BULLETS AND ONE EMPTY CHAMBER. YOU ONLY SURVIVE IF YOUR BOSS RISES.**

COOPERATE WITH YOUR COUNTERPARTS IN OTHER PARTS OF YOUR ORGANIZATION. IF THE POWER STRUCTURE CHANGES AGAINST YOU, THE PEOPLE WHO RISE REMEMBER THAT YOU WERE A GOOD GUY.

tions reversed: five bullets and one empty chamber. You only survive if your boss rises. Otherwise, you are fired or sent to Siberia.

Some of us at Commercial Credit weren't so stupid. We knew that we were holding a revolver with five bullets and one empty chamber. And the answer was, don't pull the trigger. So we simply got along with most of the staff players in other divisions. And most of us survived, even those of us whose bosses lost the race.

Cooperate with your counterparts in other parts of your organization whenever you can. Don't rumor monger. Try to accommodate them. If the power structure changes against you, the people who rise remember that you were a good guy. And you live to fight another day.

YOU WILL HAVE ENEMIES, AND THEY WILL BE UNDERHANDED

Inevitably, despite your best efforts, you will make some enemies among your peers. And by enemies, I do not mean those people who simply don't like you. I mean those people who are actively working to keep you from moving ahead.

They turn into enemies for a number of reasons.

Some of your peers will be your enemies merely because they are backing one of your rivals for the next job. The good thing about these enemies is that you can spot them easily. They are the ones who always agree with your rival in meetings, have lunch with your rival, socialize with your rival. Even a seeing-eye dog can spot them.

The most dangerous enemies among your peers, however, are not the ones who would prefer somebody else as their boss, but the ones who just don't want *you*. They can be both desperate and difficult to pick out of a crowd.

They may work against you simply because they resent not having the courage or talent or opportunity to be real contenders. Or because they know you have their number and are afraid that if you wind up as the boss, you will diminish or fire them.

Whatever their motivation for trying to block your rise, your enemies will probably not show their hand openly. Only rarely have I seen someone openly blast a peer. Once in a senior meeting, I witnessed a U-boat attack that came out of nowhere and instantly exploded. Let's call the aggressor Ned—and his intended victim Paul. "You said you were going to deliver this on that day," Ned suddenly hissed at Paul, "and you failed to do that, even though I have three memos here that said you would." Then there was cursing, there was shouting, there was name-calling.

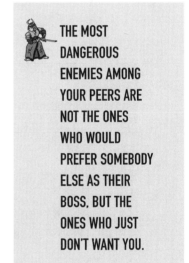

THE MOST DANGEROUS ENEMIES AMONG YOUR PEERS ARE NOT THE ONES WHO WOULD PREFER SOMEBODY ELSE AS THEIR BOSS, BUT THE ONES WHO JUST DON'T WANT YOU.

This was about the time that I started looking around and wondering, is there any more lemon Danish in the room? Because nothing good can come out of participating in a public argument like that.

I'll admit that Paul handled the attack in a very classy way. Instead of becoming defensive, he said, "I would be happy to discuss any and all of these issues, but I'm not doing it here and not doing it now because it's simply inappropriate."

Paul was right. Even if Ned was correct in principle, he did pick the wrong place, the wrong time, and the wrong tone for it. Far from doing Paul in, Ned dealt his own career a negative and unnecessary blow.

If somebody attacks you head-on, you simply have to handle yourself with aplomb. However, your more sophisticated enemies understand that assaulting you openly may mean career suicide for them.

At this level, the smart ones understand that they are not cutting down a sapling, but a mature oak that can't be done in with one swing of the ax. So they tend to use a series of small, strategic cuts over time that drain your vital sap and damage you just enough so that you are no longer the strongest choice for the job you want.

What you really have to defend against are campaigns, water-cooler campaigns, rumors that make the people in power uncomfortable with you. And generally, if your performance is good, these rumors will focus on your personal qualities.

> YOUR MORE SOPHISTICATED ENEMIES UNDERSTAND THAT THEY ARE NOT CUTTING DOWN A SAPLING, BUT A MATURE OAK THAT CAN'T BE DONE IN WITH ONE SWING OF THE AX.

For example, one of my peers once made an issue out of my "callous lack of commitment" to United Way, which, by the way, I was *not* committed to. I just wasn't callous about it. Now, United Way is clearly a good cause, and it supports a lot of very fine organizations. But I didn't like the system in some workplaces that participated in United Way, including my own.

We managers were supposed to ask our employees to contribute a regular portion of their paychecks to United Way's limited list of charities—and we competed with each other to see who could raise more money. Well, that seemed to me extraordinarily coercive and unfair. I was not going to pressure people dependent on me for every raise to change their giving patterns just so I could win some corporate do-bee contest. Giving should come from the heart, not from the coldness of a corporation's required programs.

Nonetheless, this hurt me in my boss's eyes, who thought it showed an unpleasant lack of generosity, as well as a problematic disregard for community relations. And I was only able to defend myself by walking into his office with canceled checks proving that I'd donated a great deal of money to causes that happened not to be United Way causes.

The really clever among your enemies will try to weave a theme, using a series of stories about you to illustrate why you are a risky choice for a promotion.

For a while, I had to answer a series of rumors suggesting that I was irresponsible. Some of them arrived at my boss's doors via the grapevine, others via anonymous letters (I am amazed that anyone attributes any credibility to an unsigned letter), and others via the press.

> WHAT YOU REALLY HAVE TO DEFEND AGAINST ARE CAMPAIGNS, WATER-COOLER CAMPAIGNS, RUMORS THAT MAKE THE PEOPLE IN POWER UNCOMFORTABLE WITH YOU.

For example, one of our lower-level public relations people at John Hancock once got a call from a reporter who said he'd heard that I'd been arrested on a DUI charge in Holliston, Massachusetts. I had never been to Holliston and could not find it on a map. Nonetheless, the PR people felt that they had to have the legal department look into the issue, and soon my bosses knew about it. I had to spend a day and a half saying, "Where is Holliston?" before it became apparent to everybody that there was no truth to the rumor.

> THE REALLY CLEVER AMONG YOUR ENEMIES WILL TRY TO WEAVE A THEME USING A SERIES OF STORIES ABOUT YOU.

If this kind of thing happens a few times in six months, you know that the long knives are out for you. Don't believe in coincidence.

For a campaign of rumors to be really effective, it either has to have a smidgen of truth to it—you *do* get drunk in public, just not as often as they say—or it has to be a "cross-cut" attack that undermines your self-defined strengths—you present yourself as a disciplined person who would *never* get drunk in public, but maybe you are just a hypocrite.

In presidential elections over the last 20 years, Republican political operatives have employed this cross-cut technique brilliantly. For example, when John Kerry began emphasizing his history as a highly decorated Vietnam War veteran in his 2004 presidential run, big Republican donors instantly turned this image against him. They funded a group called "Swift Boat Veterans for Truth" that disputed Kerry's accounts of heroism and unfairly painted him as a liar and an opportunist.

> FOR A CAMPAIGN OF RUMORS TO BE REALLY EFFECTIVE, IT EITHER HAS TO HAVE A SMIDGEN OF TRUTH TO IT, OR IT HAS TO BE A "CROSS-CUT" ATTACK THAT UNDERMINES YOUR SELF-DEFINED STRENGTHS.

The advantage of an attack like this is that you do half the work for your attacker. They take the energy attached to your good qualities—the time, money, and effort you've spent building a certain image—and use it against you to make you seem like a fraud. Such attacks are very common, not just in politics, but also in organizational life.

So learn to expect them, and learn how to deal with them. If you have a reputation as a good manager of people, and an enemy hears that you never say hello to the receptionist in the morning when you walk by, he may very well make that known. And because you are a candidate for higher office, everything you do is magnified. If you're a middle manager and you snub somebody? For the most part, no one cares.

Or, if you're considered really good with the finances of your business, and there begin to be some financial mistakes in your area, the worst of your peers will find a way to make sure that the top of the house hears about them.

When I was fighting for my first senior management jobs, I was considered an outgoing personality, someone a lot of people at all levels of the organization felt they could relate to. But no question, I was very direct. So a few of my peers began accusing me of being rude and disrespectful to the people I managed, my bosses began making noises about it, and it threatened to put a crimp in my upward flight.

You are going to take dents like this. While you can't escape taking them, you can't afford to take too many. So how do you fight back?

CAREFULLY REMOVE ALL TATTOOS

To fight against ugly rumors, you first have to know what's being said about you. That's not always easy. Usually, the higher you get, the more cringing yes-men you have around you. First, be smart. Place some of your trust in people who will tell you when your face is dirty, as well as when it's clean.

BE SMART. PLACE SOME OF YOUR TRUST IN PEOPLE WHO WILL TELL YOU WHEN YOUR FACE IS DIRTY, AS WELL AS WHEN IT'S CLEAN.

Second, do not give your enemies any excuses. Do not have that second drink at an office function. Be discreet. Take the risk of being somewhat private and unknown, and reveal as little as possible about your personal life. Unfair as it is, women are especially easy marks for rumors about their personal behavior because men still dominate in many organizations. If a woman is traveling a lot and goes to dinner every night with the same person of the opposite sex, that is fuel for her enemies.

Third, think about what you're best at. Anticipate cross-cut attacks that will make you seem sanctimonious or false. Anticipate also your strengths being recast as limitations. If you are an engineer, it is a good bet that at some point, some of your peers will say, "Did you actually expect creativity out of that guy? After all, he's an engineer. He's just as creative as a rock." And if you came up, as I did, from the marketing and advertising side of the business world, the criticism will always be, "He wouldn't recognize a number if it hit him over the head."

Clearly, you can't blunt criticism like this by making yourself into something you are not. But what you can do is find the very, very best people to fill in the holes. Hire a well-rounded team whose strengths are different from yours.

Fourth, accept that sometimes you just have to take the hit, the way I did on United Way, simply because you believe what you're doing is right.

Fifth, if the rumor is a lie, calmly make the facts known. If there is a crumb of truth in it, though, be humble enough to admit it and see if you can't improve yourself.

When I was accused of being rude, I used a marketing technique to address the issue. I went out and commissioned a survey of my direct

ANTICIPATE CROSS-CUT ATTACKS THAT WILL MAKE YOU SEEM SANCTIMONIOUS OR FALSE.

reports about my managerial style, a blind third-party survey with anonymous results, which I then shared with my boss and my boss's boss. I showed them that two or three people did think that I was too direct sometimes. I said, "I'm going to work on that." But they also saw that the vast majority of people who worked for me found my style refreshing and that there was no serious problem. And I won credit in their eyes just by being willing to do better.

Of course, you don't want to let a rumor throw you off your game or turn you into a transparent phony. I've watched executives who've been accused of being too far from the people do really stupid things, such as start serving food in the company cafeteria wearing a chef's hat. Seeing a senior vice president in an apron with a chef's hat on serving you chili does not necessarily increase your respect for his or her humanity. Nor does it make you want to order the chili. Everybody recognizes that it's a publicity stunt.

YOU DON'T WANT TO LET A RUMOR THROW YOU OFF YOUR GAME OR TURN YOU INTO A TRANSPARENT PHONY.

Instead of overreacting to some charge against you, recognize that just as campaigns against you gather momentum over time, you must diffuse them over time. It's not unlike tattoo removal: The laser doesn't obliterate the ink; it dissipates it, sending it back into the skin. It's about diluting the dark mark, not cutting it out. So simply try to create a more attractive impression in future.

DISCREDIT THE ENEMY

Finally, how do you deal with the enemies themselves?

First you have to flush them out. I recommended that you take a tip from the CIA on this point: Use disinformation to trick double agents into revealing themselves. Narrow your list down to the three most likely sources for any ugly story—and give each one a different piece of false information detrimental to you. Then see which piece of information surfaces.

Get scared if all three do: You are really unpopular!

What do you do when you find out who is trying to do you in? In her book *Tough Choices: A Memoir*, former Hewlett-Packard CEO Carly Fiorina tells the story of a former boss who lied about her in order to benefit one of her peers. He said that she'd regularly taken credit for somebody else's work.

Fiorina dealt with this by storming the man's office: "I startled him. . . . He started to get up. I said, 'Sit down,' and strode quickly to his desk and stood beside it as close to him as possible. I literally towered over him." After getting the man to admit she'd never taken credit for anyone else's work, she ended by telling him, "From now on, if you want to say something behind my back, you'd better be willing to say it to my face."

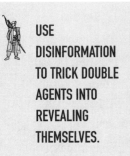

USE DISINFORMATION TO TRICK DOUBLE AGENTS INTO REVEALING THEMSELVES.

An admirably direct way of dealing with the problem—but in my experience, openly confronting an enemy and telling him that you are a good person, so cut it out, almost never works. Shame tends not to be much of a deterrent with people who are this underhanded. Knowing that you know doesn't embarrass them as much as it drives them underground and makes them even more devious.

OPENLY CONFRONTING AN ENEMY AND TELLING HIM THAT YOU ARE A GOOD PERSON, SO CUT IT OUT, ALMOST NEVER WORKS.

So what about retaliating in kind? The temptation that one has to resist is starting nasty rumors about people who've spread nasty rumors about you. This is a real test of self-discipline. If you do it, the rest of the organization sees that you are no better than your foes. So don't.

The best way to deal with a really treacherous peer is to discredit her so that the next time she says something ugly about you, it simply splashes back.

Let me tell you about my own experience with a peer who turned out to be a particularly subtle and malicious enemy. For years, I'd had these embarrassing problems. Any time I sent an e-mail critical of what was happening anywhere in the company, it would somehow find its way to the division head. Things that were supposed to be confidential regularly were not, and I wound up looking arrogant and offending people I didn't particularly want to offend.

Rumors would also surface about my temper, coloring in this portrait of arrogance. For example, I'd come into work and be amazed to learn that I'd dressed down a security guard in public the day before. It's very hard to defend yourself against stuff like this. It's like having to answer the question, "Have you stopped beating your wife?" No matter what you say, the doubt lingers.

It took me years to figure out the source of this treachery, and I could hardly believe it when I finally did: a peer who had outwardly been particularly supportive and kind. We'll call him Marty. But the truth was, Marty had been at the company long before I'd arrived, and he'd largely worked for old men who mistook him for a rising star, just because of his energy. I belonged to a different generation and thought he was a lot of bluster and relatively little substance.

Naively, I thought that all I had to do to get Marty to stop this stuff was show him I was on his side. Help him get bigger jobs, support his projects, let him take credit for more than was really warranted.

Nothing worked. Fear is a very powerful motivator, and he was simply afraid of what I would do to him if I were his boss.

Finally, I realized that the only course of action open to me was to make the rumors themselves suspect.

I'd recently been the advertising director for Michael Dukakis' 1988 presidential campaign. If the Bush victory had taught me anything, it was that

THE BEST WAY TO DEAL WITH A REALLY TREACHEROUS PEER IS TO DISCREDIT HER SO THAT THE NEXT TIME SHE SAYS SOMETHING UGLY ABOUT YOU, IT SIMPLY SPLASHES BACK.

bad information—for example, the false charge that Dukakis had been treated for a mental illness—could be just as valuable as good information in any race for the top.

So I fed Marty a lie. I told him that somebody in my division was in trouble and not going to make his numbers.

Naturally, Marty repeated this to the higher-ups at the company. When it turned out that my employee had actually performed spectacularly, Marty looked foolish. I let this happen over and over, and soon, nobody really trusted Marty when he had something unpleasant to say about me. His game had been exposed.

Mission accomplished. Of course, as soon as I became Marty's boss, I proved that he was right all along. I fired him, just as he'd always thought I would.

4

RIVALS

Defeat Them with a Siege, Not a Coup

The best revenge is massive success.

Frank Sinatra

In the old Western movies, there is often a beady-eyed undertaker there in the background, sizing up the young gunslinger and thinking, "Is this a five-foot-six coffin or a five-foot-eight coffin?"

If you are a contender for a big job, I guarantee that people are always sizing you up in the same cool way—and against your rivals, not coffin sizes.

It doesn't matter what the personality of your organization is, whether you and your rivals are jockeying for position in an atmosphere of true congeniality, or pretend congeniality, or agitation and anxiety, or open warfare. The people above you are watching how you behave with your rivals. They want to see how you handle difficult situations. And they're not above pitting you against each other—or worse, forcing you to work together.

So you have to handle your rivals intelligently, in a way that demonstrates your superior abilities as a leader. Before you can do anything smart, however, it helps to know who those rivals are. Generally, at the lower and middle levels of organizational life, you are competing against your peers. But as you rise and the circle of possible choices for every promotion tightens, you may very well be competing for the next job with anybody who's captured the attention of the big bosses and the board— including people not necessarily on your radar screen.

YOU MAY VERY WELL BE COMPETING FOR THE NEXT JOB WITH ANYBODY WHO'S CAPTURED THE ATTENTION OF THE BIG BOSSES AND THE BOARD.

Your boss is a potential rival, and so are the most visible of your own employees. Your rivals can include executives from other organizations, unfamiliar to you, who have caught somebody's eye. In a family business, the son or daughter who doesn't seem quite old enough for the job may be a rival. Your rivals can even include your own outside board members—especially those who are semiretired or in a job that's smaller than the one opening up.

In this era of corporate scandal and management upheaval, a number of outside directors at different organizations have been drafted into the executive suite as interim CEOs, only to become permanent. And this has probably not escaped the notice of your board members.

Some of them may be getting ready themselves to say, reluctantly, "If you draft me, I'll do it." Meanwhile, they may have been actively campaigning for the job for years.

ONE EXTRA SLICE OF PEPPERONI CAN ALTER YOUR ENTIRE CAREER. SO START BUILDING A REPUTATION FOR LEADERSHIP TODAY.

This happened to someone I knew who was in line for a CEO's job, a woman we'll call Kate. Kate noticed one of her board members often having lunch with other senior executives without her and also spending an unusual amount of time with the CFO. It finally dawned on her that this board member was vying for the CEO's spot, too.

So Kate launched a study about the board's conflicts of interest. While it was known that the board member in question was also a vendor to the company, Kate's "study" pointed out the conflict as a growing concern. And the board forced her would-be rival out.

Your rivals aren't under every rock, but they are behind an awful lot of desks.

ALLOW YOUR RIVALS TO BE SHORT-SIGHTED

In all contests for a big job, he whose timing is best wins.

This means a few things. First, you have to understand that the race is always on, even if you see no immediate opening above you, because you cannot predict when a power shift will occur. Somebody gets killed in a hunting accident, and suddenly you have a chance at the job you've always coveted. This actually happened to me. And no, I wasn't hunting that day.

Or somebody is abruptly done in by a scandal or wakes up one morning finally ready to open that B&B in Vermont. Somebody else intends to retire in three years but is done in by a heart attack. One extra slice of pepperoni can alter your entire career. So start building a reputation for leadership today.

On the other hand, be aware that races for the top handful of positions in any organization are, generally speaking, long—three, five, seven years. They're not tomorrow. It's far better to be a steady incremental player who wins, in the end, by impressing people all along the way than to be the kind of hothead who tries to force a quick culmination.

> **IT'S FAR BETTER TO BE A STEADY INCREMENTAL PLAYER WHO WINS, IN THE END, BY IMPRESSING PEOPLE ALL ALONG THE WAY THAN TO BE THE KIND OF HOTHEAD WHO TRIES TO FORCE A QUICK CULMINATION.**

The less intelligent among your rivals will do just that. They will destroy their chances long term in order to beat you today.

Those rivals who are openly political definitely fall into this category. They're throwing darts at you at meetings, whispering in your boss's ear. The political players are relatively easy to defeat because they almost always overplay their hand and do themselves in.

Others may actually be dumb enough to undermine the goals of the business in order to beat you. I remember working with a really ambitious information technology executive who was in line for the same job I was. Let's call him Tom. Tom was probably second only to payroll in terms of the amount of money he controlled. So I had a hundred projects in his shop at any given time, and it was like working with a general contractor on a new house: Everything comes in 30 percent over budget and takes twice as long as promised, and the kitchen is still not finished, yet the guy is completely evasive when confronted. Actually, it was like working with a bad general contractor on about a hundred houses, with a hundred unfinished kitchens, simultaneously.

And, of course, the world of IT is so esoteric that anytime anybody complained, Tom would give some excuse that would have everybody scratching their heads: "Our capacity is only ten gazillion megabytes, and we really need to be at twenty gazillion megabytes."

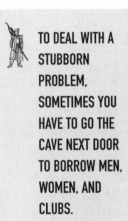

TO DEAL WITH A STUBBORN PROBLEM, SOMETIMES YOU HAVE TO GO THE CAVE NEXT DOOR TO BORROW MEN, WOMEN, AND CLUBS.

The truth was, Tom wanted to rise. And he'd decided to rise by holding his rivals' projects hostage. Corporate life. Hollywood's got nothing on it for treachery.

For a long time, Tom won all the battles. To deal with a stubborn problem like this, sometimes you have to go the cave next door to borrow men, women, and clubs. So I finally went to some of my other rivals and convinced them that we needed to put our own differences aside in order to get rid of Tom. As I said earlier, killing off somebody at this level is basically like chopping down a redwood. You have to do it one stroke at a time. One person had to go and complain about how slow and overpriced the IT work was, then another person, and then another.

Finally, it got to a point where the ultimate boss couldn't take the complaints anymore. He woke up one morning and said, "You know, I'm going to kill that IT guy." And Tom was gone so fast! Cremated, no coffin.

Nearly as short-sighted as undermining the business in order to win a promotion is goosing the business artificially for a short-term effect. I have seen more executives take out this petard and blow themselves up with it than almost any other. They'll do anything—anything reasonably legal—to make great numbers right before a job opens up. They'll push their sales forces brutally hard. They'll count all the revenue they can, including some revenue that actually should be booked for next quarter.

Well, the wonderful thing about quarters is that they end. The bad news is, the new quarter starts the next day.

By then, everybody's spent. There's nothing left in the coffers. There's nothing left in terms of people's energy. And maybe the opening that was supposed to appear doesn't. Yeah, somebody was going to retire—but then, sometimes, a mind gets changed. You can't always predict when it's going to happen. So trying to inflate your numbers in the expectation that you're going to hit the quarter just right is as silly as a football coach saying, "Let's score all the touchdowns in the first half and hope the other team doesn't score any in the second half."

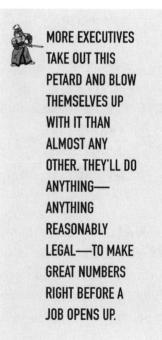

MORE EXECUTIVES TAKE OUT THIS PETARD AND BLOW THEMSELVES UP WITH IT THAN ALMOST ANY OTHER. THEY'LL DO ANYTHING—ANYTHING REASONABLY LEGAL—TO MAKE GREAT NUMBERS RIGHT BEFORE A JOB OPENS UP.

Equally short-sighted is trying to bribe your team with big bonuses to win their loyalty, a political player's way to keep a political base. Using compensation as a political tool usually backfires because you generally can't keep giving everybody huge amounts of money every year. Soon the empire gets too big, and you have to spread it too far. And suddenly, your formerly loyal lieutenants are grumbling and have decided to help somebody else win the big job.

A lot of short-term rivals wind up being short term by doing dumb things. These contests are not coups, generally. They are sieges. So time is on your side. Relax and behave like a leader.

PATIENTLY PROVE THAT YOU ARE BETTER

One of the smartest ways to get the better of your rivals is not to engage them and certainly not to attack them directly, but just to look good by contrast.

It helps to be aware of what your rival's weaknesses are. Your objective is not to exploit a weakness by embarrassing the rival. Your objective is simply to show that you don't have any similar weakness. To do that, you may have to share more than you're used to with the people above you.

I can remember having a rival who had a very senior subordinate with a terrible alcohol problem. My rival decided to get rid of the person, quietly. Alcoholism was never discussed—his job was just eliminated.

USING COMPENSATION AS A POLITICAL TOOL USUALLY BACKFIRES.

Now, in most organizations, the people at the very top really do believe that they are benevolent despots and prefer not to think of their organization as so very cold-hearted. So when I had a similar problem, I went out, hired a counselor and a psychiatrist, and walked my employee through months of recovery, to the point of sending him away to a rehabilitation center at company expense. I thought this person was worth the trouble, and I was preserving a company asset.

But I also kept my bosses informed, allowing them to make the comparison between me and my rival—and to discover that I did not share his desire to sweep problems under the rug. It also didn't hurt that I'd reinforced their benevolent self-image.

NEVER UNDERESTIMATE THE POWER OF THE POINTED QUESTION

Of course, it may benefit you now and then, not just to provide instructive contrast, but also to actively alert your boss to your rivals' shortcomings. Gossip is not the way to go. Knowledge is. Use your allies to help you gather information, and demonstrate your superior knowledge of your rival's business.

Let me give you an example from my career: I was at one company when a rival who ran international relations for us—let's call him Sean—gave a presentation about a new business he wanted to launch in Southeast Asia. Sean intended to spend $200 million on it.

IT HELPS TO BE AWARE OF WHAT YOUR RIVAL'S WEAKNESSES ARE.

Now, protocol was that you never, ever questioned a rival at what I call "show- and-tell" meetings—those meetings where everybody gives a presentation about his or her department or division in front of the top executives. Meetings like these tend to be as uncritical as a kindergarten show-and-tell, where everybody is expected to "ooh" and "ah" whether the person sharing has brought in something truly interesting, like a two-headed salamander, or a washcloth. Organizational etiquette can be truly foolish at times, and sometimes you need to risk breaking the rules.

TO ALERT YOUR BOSS TO YOUR RIVALS' SHORTCOMINGS, GOSSIP IS NOT THE WAY TO GO. KNOWLEDGE IS.

So I said, "My understanding is that our competitors are going to spend on average a billion dollars entering this market." Sean hadn't mentioned this fact, but I'd studied before I got there. "So why will we be successful spending just $200 million?"

His answer was flip and arrogant, both bad traits to display in a formal meeting: "Because we're smarter than the competition."

"I think we are smarter," I said carefully. "There's no question in my mind that we're smarter than our competition. The question is, are we *five times* as smart?"

Was that polite of me? It was barely within the rules of engagement. And it did not endear me to my rival. But I'd asked where the beef was, and nobody in a position of power ever forgot it. They went home that night worrying, "We just approved something where we're spending a fifth of our competition. Are we five times as smart?"

After that moment, every time Sean came to a meeting and said how well his business was doing, the president would ask, "Well, how's our competition doing?" That question was now omnipresent. Sure enough, when the business began to falter a year or so later, I got credit for having predicted it.

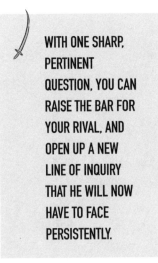

WITH ONE SHARP, PERTINENT QUESTION, YOU CAN RAISE THE BAR FOR YOUR RIVAL, AND OPEN UP A NEW LINE OF INQUIRY THAT HE WILL NOW HAVE TO FACE PERSISTENTLY.

With one sharp, pertinent question, you can raise the bar for your rival, open up a new line of inquiry that he will now have to face persistently, and begin to control the dynamic in management meetings.

And you'll probably have the field all to yourself in this game, since most of your rivals won't avail themselves of a similar opportunity to ask questions about your work. They will be too lazy or too busy worrying about their own world to demonstrate any interest in what you're doing. Or they will lack the fundamental courage to question you, or they will think it's just poor form.

My reaction to the form issue is that as long as you're not overly aggressive and obviously trying to poke at a rival, it's okay. You don't ask too embarrassing a question, and you don't ask too personal a question. Instead, you ask a business question that demonstrates your breadth of knowledge about the organization—and the degree to which you have the organization's best interests at heart. You don't do it every time by any means, just now and then.

So, go ahead, ask one, penetrating, smart question of a rival. Ask precisely the kind of question that a boss might ask.

Of course, you can only play this game for residual strength. It won't work if you have big holes in your own portfolio. All the pieces you're in charge of will have to be clicking—that's a given.

It won't be effective, either, if every time something comes out of your mouth it's detrimental to your rival. So, if you happen to be in a meeting in which a contender reports that she has done something remarkable, behave like a grown-up. Most people won't compliment a rival in front of the boss. But when you are in a meeting in which a rival says, "I'm 140 percent over my sales projections," the appropriate response is an expression of respect or admiration. If you are silent, people know you're jealous. Never show you're jealous. Not ever. Bite your tongue until it is black and blue first. And make sure that the compliments are genuine and flow properly.

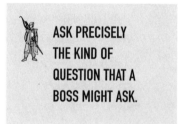

ASK PRECISELY THE KIND OF QUESTION THAT A BOSS MIGHT ASK.

The truth is, with compliments and questions, what you are really doing is giving your rivals a performance appraisal in public. You are subtly demonstrating how terrific you would be as their boss—and hopefully, planting this idea in the minds of the decision makers.

IF YOU CAN'T RESIST A SHOW OF AGGRESSION, MAKE SURE IT'S LETHAL

Sometimes, however, your rivals will irk you or threaten you enough that you simply cannot resist shooting at them. I have one piece of advice for you: If you must shoot, do not shoot to wound. Finish the person off as a rival.

For example, in New York I once had a rival who was a very smart guy, a very talented executive. Let's call him Harry. I had recommended Harry for a job running one of the organization's businesses because I thought he would be good for it and it would be good for him.

Unfortunately, Harry ended up building an impossibly cliquish team. They had their own logo, and they came to work every day wearing these logo pins on their suit jackets. Their disregard for the larger organization carried over into their work style, too. They were difficult to deal with, since they thought they were better than the rest of us. If this weren't grating enough, I also learned that Harry had taken a lot of shots at me, privately, with the powers that be.

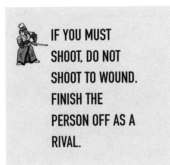

IF YOU MUST SHOOT, DO NOT SHOOT TO WOUND. FINISH THE PERSON OFF AS A RIVAL.

Then I went to a three-day meeting with the company's management team of 150 people at some off-site casual-dress resort. Harry and his group all appeared at the "get acquainted" bar-beque on the first night wearing matching navy blue jackets with a logo patch. They'd also given these jackets to three or four of the big bosses, who all wore them.

So there we were, 130 of us in street clothes and 20 in uniform. It was completely antithetical to the goal of the meeting, which was to make the company more, not less, cohesive. It was also vaguely insulting to anybody who didn't rate a blue jacket.

The barbeque was on a Wednesday night. I knew that Harry was scheduled to present on Thursday, and I was scheduled to present on Friday morning. So here is what I did.

I borrowed one of the jackets from somebody Thursday morning, promising to have it back in time for the dinner that night so that no one would know who the traitor was. Then I had it hustled 90 miles back to New York, where I had our audiovisual team put together a *60 Minutes* parody, complete with ticking clock, concerned correspondent, and whistle-blowing scientist. The piece was an exposé on a manufacturing defect in the jackets that caused them to explode, and it ended with a very funny montage of entire landscapes going up in flames.

I used this video clip to begin my presentation Friday morning, and it was a sensation. People gasped in shock that I'd been able to pull off something so pointed so quickly. And then they roared, particularly those sans jackets.

That night, right from the meeting, I left for a long-scheduled trip to Europe. When I got back 10 days later, my jacket video was still the talk of the company. Harry was furious, furious, furious. And the chairman called me into his office and just eviscerated me, interrupting, of course, every few minutes to say, "That was the funniest thing I've ever seen. But don't *ever* do anything like it again."

Now, if my performance had been down and I hadn't been making my numbers, I'd have done my presentation as straight as an arrow. You can only pull off a stunt like this if your own house is in impeccable order.

But we were doing well, so I took a risk. I knew that my video was not a firing offense, so I was willing to take what was clearly going to be a hit from my superiors to make a point. I hadn't attacked Harry personally, but I did point out a problem with his attitude toward the company as a whole, something the big bosses should have done much earlier. And I'd done it with some humor, which makes many an aggressive move more forgivable.

> IF MY PERFORMANCE HAD BEEN DOWN AND I HADN'T BEEN MAKING MY NUMBERS, I'D HAVE DONE MY PRESENTATION AS STRAIGHT AS AN ARROW. BUT WE WERE DOING WELL, SO I TOOK A RISK.

Interestingly enough, not too long afterward, this rival was no longer a rival at all. Harry was sent to work for me. No problem. He was a very talented guy, and I was happy to have him on my team.

HANDLING A SNAKE IN YOUR OWN NEST

You may be a great person, a benevolent person, and a kind person, and your employees may appreciate that. But understand that nobody likes being told what to do. I didn't like my parents telling me what to do, and they were my parents—let alone some stranger who through an accident of fate happened to be my boss.

So try not to be too, too surprised if you get the sense that somebody who works for you wants to become your boss. If he is just ambitious and not trying to undermine you, fine. You can use him to your advantage. He'll work like a dog to prove himself.

> **TRY NOT TO BE TOO, TOO SURPRISED IF YOU GET THE SENSE THAT SOMEBODY WHO WORKS FOR YOU WANTS TO BECOME YOUR BOSS.**

If he is trying to undermine you, on the other hand, by saying bad things about you behind your back and trying to negotiate with the other powers in the organization, then you have to fire him. You don't transfer—you fire him. Never on performance, ever, because presumably he is doing well. So eliminate his job, split the job in two, whatever it takes. Make sure that it is a complete surprise, too, so that he has no time to launch a defense that might damage you.

Just walk in one morning and get rid of him. People like this are too impatient to wait their turn, and it is tough enough trying to watch your back against attacks from outside enemies. But attacks from your own people? I don't think so.

IF YOU ARE THE SNAKE IN THE NEST, STRIKE QUICKLY

Earlier, I said that most rivalries are sieges. There is an exception, however. If you decide that you are going to take your boss's job from her, that is a coup.

Act quickly, before her paranoia has a chance to flower, because dawdling is dangerous. Your boss has more access than you do to the CEO and the board. She could easily plant so much kindling wood under you, it would make Joan of Arc look like a marshmallow roast.

But if you have done a good job with the people above your boss, and you sense that your boss is just gliding, and you also sense that people at the top know it, make your move.

IF YOU LOSE TO YOUR RIVAL, EITHER LEARN TO LIKE EATING CROW, OR GO

I've never believed in being overly friendly with my rivals—or even terribly polite. Civil, yes. Friendly, no. And that's because by the time I reached the middle levels of organizational life, I saw no reason whatsoever to curry favor with my competitors.

I'd already made the decision that I wasn't going to work for any of them. I'd leave first, because I didn't want to stay in the organization having lost the race.

If you do stay on as a loser, you generally either have to find another place to go within the organization that offers you another chance to rise, or wait out your rival's tenure—five years, seven years, ten years—for a second shot at the job you wanted. That is a lot of time if you are in your 40s or 50s.

Even if you do wait it out, getting the job will be that much harder on the next go 'round. First, you have already been found lacking once. And second, the rival who won the job now gets to influence who comes in after him.

Still, sometimes the people who wait it out do get second chances. Less than two years after Andrea Jung was passed

 MOST RIVALRIES ARE SIEGES. HOWEVER, IF YOU DECIDE THAT YOU ARE GOING TO TAKE YOUR BOSS'S JOB FROM HER, THAT IS A COUP.

over for the CEO's job at Avon in favor of an outsider, she was named CEO. Of course, she was only 39 years old when she lost out on the top job. Time was on her side, so she stuck around and prevailed in the end.

However, the outcome of the succession race at General Electric in 2000 is more typical. Within eight days of Jack Welch's announcement that Jeffrey Immelt had won the race, Immelt's two rivals had left for other organizations, Robert Nardelli to run Home Depot and W. James McNerney, Jr., to run 3M.

Clearly, they were not going to stay on as losers reporting to their former rival even for a minute.

There are very, very few real contenders who can bear to report to a former rival, no matter what leaving costs them in terms of deferred compensation and pensions.

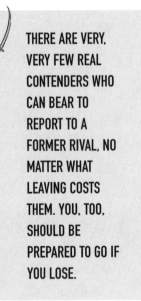

THERE ARE VERY, VERY FEW REAL CONTENDERS WHO CAN BEAR TO REPORT TO A FORMER RIVAL, NO MATTER WHAT LEAVING COSTS THEM. YOU, TOO, SHOULD BE PREPARED TO GO IF YOU LOSE.

You, too, should be prepared to go if you lose.

Why do I say that? Because, if you are truly ambitious, you are unlikely to be happy if you stay. It's not just about the closing off of opportunities, the loss of the bigger money and the bigger responsibility. It's also about the slow slide, the humiliation, the death by a thousand cuts.

Generally, when your rival first triumphs, you two have dinner, and you promise to be good to each other, for the children's sake.

But the first day you have to walk into her office, and she's sitting behind the big desk, and you're sitting in the chair in front of the big desk—that's hard. Your expense account now has to be signed by her. She gets to pick where you go to lunch. She gets to pick everything. And when she speaks in a meeting, you have to shut down. The empress has conquered your kingdom. She may have left you your army, but you now have to kiss her ring.

Even your loyal army may not quite give you the respect they once did. Now that the race is lost, they know that their fate, for the most part, is no longer in your hands. You have another problem, too, which is that your rival's loyal lieutenants now have more power than you do. And you're cooling your heels waiting outside the new executive vice president's office while her staff people are whizzing in and out.

It doesn't matter that you still have 50,000 people reporting to you. You lost. And everybody knows. Your staff knows. Your kids know. Your mother could have Alzheimer's, but she'd still know enough to ask, "Didn't you get that job?"

IF YOU REALLY BELIEVE THAT YOU'RE MEANT TO RUN SOMETHING, GO RUN SOMETHING.

And if you've been working together with your rival for a long time and your families are connected, it can be hard on them, too. Maybe your spouses used to play golf together, and your kids used to get together for play dates. Now your spouse thinks he or she has to wait for the other spouse to call. A lot of this stuff is very personal. It's why rivals seldom end up as lasting friends.

In short, working for a former rival is very, very hard on the ego.

If your ego is one that says, "I can't subjugate myself," then you can't do it. So don't.

If you really believe that you're meant to run something, go run something. Maybe it's smaller, and maybe it's less prestigious than the organization you were hoping to run, but go run something anyway—and make it bigger and more prestigious. You will be happier, and it will be better for your career in the long run.

WITH FORMER RIVALS, IT'S KISS OR KILL

If you win the race, it's either embrace your rivals or kill them. There's nothing in between, because nothing is more dangerous than allowing the defeated to remain rivals.

The way Nicholas J. Nicholas handled his long-time rival Gerald Levin at Time, Inc., offers a great example of what not to do. When Nicholas was in ascendance in the mid-1980s, he took over Levin's role as head of the video group, and Levin was moved aside into a rather empty position in "strategy." Then a few months after Nicholas was named to the presidency in 1986, Levin was further diminished by being kicked off the board. In Richard M. Clurman's book, *To the End of Time: The Seduction and Conquest of a Media Empire,* Nicholas explains, "Did I agree with the decision? Absolutely.... My betting was that Jerry was not going to stay."

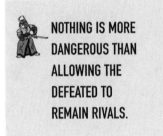

NOTHING IS MORE DANGEROUS THAN ALLOWING THE DEFEATED TO REMAIN RIVALS.

But Nicholas didn't get rid of him once and for all, and Levin did stay and made his way back into power. In 1992, after the merger between Time and Warner, Levin engineered the ouster of Nicholas and took the CEO's job away from him. Surprise, surprise.

Again, don't shoot to wound. If you want to take out a former rival, in most cases, it's safest to just take him out. That's why so few organizations choose a ranch house for their headquarters. The headquarters are all in tall buildings so that former rivals can be thrown off the roof.

That said, once you have killed somebody off, put your six-shooter away. It's unseemly to keep plugging away at the body. Don't denigrate the person; let him leave with dignity. Take a lesson from the career of Eliot Spitzer, the crusading attorney general who was elected governor of New York State in 2006. While he did a lot of good in fighting the excesses of Wall Street, it seemed never to be enough for him to simply win his point. He continued humiliating his targets even after extracting his pound of flesh. It's not surprising that almost nobody suggested that Spitzer deserved any mercy, either, when he was caught patronizing expensive prostitutes. Within days of this revelation, he was forced to resign.

And if you actually need the abilities of a former rival and want to hang on to the person, do not be stupid. Give him respect.

I always thought it was a good idea, for example, when I had to meet with a rival who lost, to go to his office the first few times. And then, if he was coming to see me, I would come out of my office to greet him.

Ameliorating the humiliation by any means you can is extraordinarily important. You have to be careful socially. Don't allow your spouse to lord it over the rival's spouse.

FEW ORGANIZATIONS CHOOSE A RANCH HOUSE FOR THEIR HEADQUARTERS. THE HEADQUARTERS ARE ALL IN TALL BUILDINGS SO THAT FORMER RIVALS CAN BE THROWN OFF THE ROOF.

No matter how careful you are, you'll have mixed success because most of your rivals really believe that they deserved the job and that you didn't. Some people will tell you straight out, "I don't know how you beat me." Other people will say all the right things, but their behavior is undermining or difficult. Or they can't get rid of their anger or disappointment. There is no point in discussing it with them. It's not your problem. They just have to go.

On the other hand, one of the most disappointed people I've ever beaten in a race turned out to be one of my best employees. Let's call him Clark. For the longest time, Clark was the golden boy at this company where I worked.

Everyone expected him to get the brass ring and run a major division. He was smart, articulate, knew the numbers. Some thought his people skills were a bit lacking, but he was clearly the hare in the race. And I was the tortoise who just kept building a group of highly capable people and getting results. And when the time came, I'm sure it was a tough decision for the powers-that-be, but Clark lost.

IF YOU NEED THE ABILITIES OF A FORMER RIVAL AND WANT TO HANG ON TO THE PERSON, DO NOT BE STUPID. GIVE HIM RESPECT.

He was clearly angry. So I just left him alone for three months, except to ask his opinions and treat him respectfully.

After awhile, he realized that, at age 52, he'd probably gone as high in his career as he was likely to go. This is not unlike an aging Major League pitcher realizing, "Gee, I can still throw the ball at 90 miles an hour, but for some reason, they can hit it now." And Clark made a personal decision to accept that reality gracefully.

So he came around, and he was great.

That's the thing about real rivals. The best of them are as impressive as you are. Don't forget it when you're running against them, and don't forget it when you win.

THE TEAM YOU ASSEMBLE

You Risk Your Reputation with Every Hire and Fire

A man is known by the company he organizes.

Ambrose Bierce

How important are the people who report to you? Think of it this way: One's your liver, one's your heart, one's your stomach, another is your eyes or your ears. No matter how high an opinion you have of yourself, you cannot survive without your vital organs.

The more you rise, the more you need good people to work for you. You need them simply to help you achieve your goals and make sure that your base is covered. But you also need them to be seen as a positive force in the organization and to advertise your effectiveness. You need them to say positive things about you, for the most part, and spread the word about your abilities as a leader.

So, to reach the upper echelons of organizational life, you have to be able to attract real talent and then handle that talent in such a way that people will do their best for you and speak well of you. In this chapter, we'll talk about building a team of people who will help you rise—and in the next chapter, we'll talk about motivating those people to give you their all.

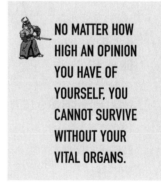

NO MATTER HOW HIGH AN OPINION YOU HAVE OF YOURSELF, YOU CANNOT SURVIVE WITHOUT YOUR VITAL ORGANS.

My first piece of advice in assembling a team is to choose wisely because you are being watched.

NOBODY TOOK THE GABOR SISTERS SERIOUSLY, EITHER

In the middle levels of organizational life, you can hide the mistakes you make in hiring, firing, and promoting simply by being a terrific performer yourself. In the upper levels of organizational life, that is no longer possible.

The people who report to you now are relatively senior themselves and much more visible than your other employees ever were. They are certainly going to be exposed to other executives in the organization and possibly to your president or CEO. They may very well have contact with your board of directors. They are wearing your brand, even if you inherited rather than picked them.

Former Disney Chairman Michael Eisner succinctly sums up what's at issue here in the autobiography he wrote with Tony Schwartz, *Work in Progress: Risking Failure, Surviving Success*: "Executives can be judged on many qualities, but high on my list is how well they hire. Insecure managers invariably choose weak, nonthreatening subordinates. Confident managers hire the best people they can find, aware that improving overall performance will ultimately redound to their credit."

> IF YOU HIRE FOOLS OR LUNATICS, PEOPLE WILL START TO WORRY THAT YOU MAY BE FOOLISH OR CRAZY YOURSELF.

Let me extend this idea further: If you hire fools or lunatics, well, people will start to worry that you may be foolish or crazy yourself. And they might be right!

The truth is that you are allowed a certain number of personnel mistakes as you rise, but not many. It's similar to the difference between somebody who's been divorced and somebody who's been divorced as often as a Gabor sister, those three fixtures of mid-twentieth-century Hollywood who ran through 20 husbands among them.

In the first case, well, the person has made a mistake or two—we're all only human. In the second case, you start to look at the person and think, "*You're* the problem."

WHEN IT COMES TO OUTSIDERS, MEASURE TWICE, CUT ONCE

Every personnel choice you make in upper management is risky, but especially risky is bringing in a senior person from outside the organization.

You are subjecting the group to new DNA—inserting a fish gene into a tomato, in effect—and people view the end result with the same suspicion. There's an automatic resentment of your outsider because he or she obviously took the job away from someone on the inside. People will inevitably question what level of knowledge your person really has.

In one of my first senior management jobs, I hired a woman who had an impeccable résumé, just impeccable. She appeared to be a top-notch manager, and I needed her to manage a lot of people. She came from an Ivy League school. I interviewed her twice, a bit of a straight-laced personality, but she seemed very competent. Her references were great, too, and she'd come from a highly reputable company.

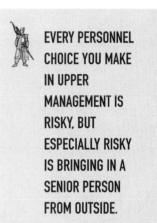

EVERY PERSONNEL CHOICE YOU MAKE IN UPPER MANAGEMENT IS RISKY, BUT ESPECIALLY RISKY IS BRINGING IN A SENIOR PERSON FROM OUTSIDE.

Of course, the reason nobody there would say anything bad about her was because they were so desperate to get rid of her.

Not only was her work remarkably shabby and inaccurate, her behavior was so bizarre that she soon lost all credibility with the people who worked for her.

Here is just one example among many: She had this strange relationship with M&Ms. She would buy a giant bag of M&Ms, and instead of having lunch, she would take them into a conference room and lay them all out, by color, battalions of M&Ms, all with the letter "M" facing her. Never mind the sanitary issues of eating them right off the conference table, she'd *talk* to her candies before she ate them: "Okay, yellow battalion, your turn!"

So I had to go to my superiors and say, "She's really not working out." I talked about her bad performance. Then, to prove the need to fire her quickly, I made the mistake of telling them the M&M story.

Their first question was, "Where did you *find* somebody like that?"

It was not about her—it was about me! Very embarrassing. That is why a lot of executives prefer to find a team by promoting from within an organization. It's often safer to choose the devil you know.

My advice is not to avoid hiring from outside at all costs but to be very deliberate in assembling your team. When I've made my mistakes, it's been because I moved too quickly. I panicked over the fact that I had a problem in some area and hired somebody without enough due diligence.

It's not easy to get a bead on a potential employee. Résumé writing these days is an art. I can't tell you how many people I've interviewed who all claimed that they single-handedly turned Fidelity Investments into the giant it is today.

References are also not very reliable. People are so afraid of being sued that it's very hard to get an honest answer about a person's capabilities, so you have to listen carefully for any hint that the candidate is being damned with faint praise. Headhunters' opinions are generally not much more valuable. Most are much more interested in collecting fees than they are in giving you an honest assessment of the people they send to you.

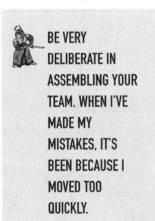

BE VERY DELIBERATE IN ASSEMBLING YOUR TEAM. WHEN I'VE MADE MY MISTAKES, IT'S BEEN BECAUSE I MOVED TOO QUICKLY.

So take in all this information, and then make a few phone calls yourself to the world at large to try to get a pattern on a person. Spend time with the person. Have some of your staff members you respect spend time with the candidate, too, and then compare notes.

You might assume that because the people you are interviewing have reached a certain level, they are capable. Don't assume any such thing. Finding talent with a well-written résumé is relatively easy. Finding capable talent is hard. Capable of fitting in. Capable of fitting in quickly. Capable of hitting the ground running.

If you are interviewing someone outside your area of expertise, which you will find yourself doing more frequently as you rise, have somebody who is an expert interview the candidate, too. For example, I wouldn't know a good information technology person if God put her across the table from me. I'd leave that judgment up to technology people I trust.

Choose carefully, particularly outsiders, because getting rid of somebody at the levels we are now talking about is no longer a casual matter. It is a big deal. It may even make it into the newspapers. As a result, those meetings where you have to explain to your superiors why you want to get rid of somebody you brought into the organization are generally an inquisition.

You may very well hear something like this: "You just hired this person a year ago. You told us this person had a great résumé. What changed? You do remember, don't you, that we just spent $200,000 on the headhunter's fee to get this person?"

> FINDING TALENT WITH A WELL-WRITTEN RÉSUMÉ IS RELATIVELY EASY. FINDING CAPABLE TALENT IS HARD.

It can get worse: "In the last three years, you have hired seven people from the outside at senior-level positions, and three of them are gone. Is it really them, or is it you? Is it that you are difficult to work for, or do you just make bad choices? Maybe next time we should interview your candidate, too."

Make too many bad choices, and not only will you suffer a loss of face, but also a loss of power. You will start getting more "help" with these personnel decisions and find yourself constantly second-guessed. And the very last thing you want is to have people forced on you.

GOOD PEOPLE CAN STILL COST YOU

It's not just the incompetent or crazy hires who can hurt you. You can also be hurt by somebody who is actually doing a good job but presents badly or has otherwise made a bad impression on your CEO or board of directors. When I was CEO of John Hancock, I once attended a conference in Italy with an executive who was a big star for me. Let's call him Pete. He was in his mid-40s and somebody to whom I wanted to give a huge chunk of additional responsibilities. But Pete had reached the level where he had to become more familiar to the board members before he could move any higher.

It was the perfect environment. We were in Rome, thousands of miles from the office. It was a free night from the conference, so I arranged for a very influential board member and his wife to have dinner with Pete and me. The board member wasn't quite a king-maker, but he did have enough power to stop a prince he didn't like.

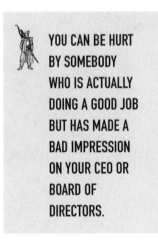

YOU CAN BE HURT BY SOMEBODY WHO IS ACTUALLY DOING A GOOD JOB BUT HAS MADE A BAD IMPRESSION ON YOUR CEO OR BOARD OF DIRECTORS.

We had a drink at the dinner table, we ordered a bottle of wine, and everything was going swimmingly. Then we reached the *primi piatti*, and Pete suddenly dropped his face into the truffles and tagliatelle and completely passed out.

It turned out that he was so nervous about meeting the board member that he'd had three martinis at the hotel before dinner. I think those were the most expensive martinis anyone has ever ordered. They were a career-croaker for him. I had to tell the guy the next morning, "I'm happy to have you stay in your job, but you are not going anyplace now."

And that nosedive into the pasta made me look like an idiot. I had to spend the next year being careful about all my personnel moves.

Given their increasing sense of personal liability since the Enron scandal, outside board members are bolder and bolder in questioning personnel decisions. They are more likely to be highly critical of any of your hires who make it onto their radar. They are more likely to block the advancement of anyone they don't like—or even force you to throw the person overboard.

And it's always *your* judgment that's in question.

Of course, things can be even worse when the board or the CEO grows to really like one of your people, and *you* decide that the person is doing a poor job. In that case, you probably have to prove that he is failing to your superiors—your aghast and disbelieving superiors—before you'll get the go-ahead to get rid of him.

I once had a finance person who was a great presenter but really technically incompetent. He made mistakes all the time—clearly, a serious liability to me. But he was loyal as a Labrador. He never said a bad word about me, never complained, took whatever raise I gave him. A supremely nice guy, and he was highly regarded by many people in the organization.

GIVEN THEIR INCREASING SENSE OF PERSONAL LIABILITY SINCE THE ENRON SCANDAL, OUTSIDE BOARD MEMBERS ARE BOLDER AND BOLDER IN QUESTIONING PERSONNEL DECISIONS.

I wasn't eager to fire him since I had just recently made a few other core personnel moves, including a firing. So I came up with a solution that made everybody happy: I traded him to an enemy and let him make his errors elsewhere. Then he got fired by someone else.

INSIST ON YOUR OWN PICKS

You are going to be judged on the quality of your team, no matter what, so don't assume that you will be given a pass just because somebody is forced on you. Once I ended up managing a senior employee who was very friendly with the president of the organization. Let's call him Jerry. I realized that Jerry was an obstruction who had to go—but I didn't know how to take him out without getting the president to agree.

Each year this company did a review of all the executives in a division with five key board members and the chairman. At the review of my group, a very senior outside director turned to me and surprised me with two pointed questions: "Does Jerry really know his business? Does he make his goals every quarter?"

I had to answer "No" to both.

"Well, this is a very key position," he said. "Don't you think it's irresponsible not to fire him?"

Presumably, a slightly horrified expression crossed my face because the chairman now winked at me. And I instantly knew what had happened.

SIMPLY INSIST, "I PICK MY OWN TEAM." THAT'S BALLSY, BUT IT'S SAFER THAN THE ALTERNATIVE.

The chairman had teed up the whole thing. He agreed with me about Jerry but didn't want me to discuss Jerry's shortcomings with the president because a cloak of protection would have instantly gone up around the guy.

So now I had to fire Jerry. And the one thing I'd been trying to avoid in not firing Jerry—making a lifelong enemy of the organization's president—happened anyway. That taught me a few very valuable lessons. First, to take my punishment early. What I should have done was get rid of Jerry as soon as I understood he was unproductive and spared myself this embarrassing hour with the board.

Second, I should have fought for the right person for Jerry's job rather than accept someone who was handed to me. I have worked in many organizations where the kings want to move the players around underneath you. Resist. Simply insist, "I pick my own team."

Now, that's ballsy, but it's safer than the alternative. Because if you are not picking your own team, it's quite likely that you are going to be handed some turkeys. When one of those turkeys screws up, you now own the turkey. It's not the king's fault; *you* are the bad manager.

Unlike you, the king has the right to selective memory: "I don't recall participating in the decision to promote that person," he can claim. And having the facts on your side will not help you in the least.

DO NOT BUILD AN ARMY OF CLONES

Ever notice how some departments have people who look, sound, and act just like the boss? They all run marathons, like the boss. They all buy their clothes at Brooks Brothers, like the boss. They all write the same style of memo, like the boss. It's not a coincidence.

The truth is that when you are the boss, it's really hard to hire people unlike yourself, either in personality or in expertise. Why? Because they can make you ill at ease.

Do it anyway if you think they are right for the job. Personally, I tend to get along better with creative people than with financial people. And I tend to get along better with financial people than with technologists. But you will reach a point where you will need all of them, so go out of your way to judge people who are unlike you fairly. Otherwise, your performance will suffer.

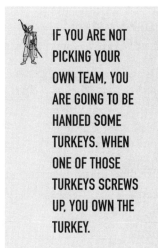

IF YOU ARE NOT PICKING YOUR OWN TEAM, YOU ARE GOING TO BE HANDED SOME TURKEYS. WHEN ONE OF THOSE TURKEYS SCREWS UP, YOU OWN THE TURKEY.

And for God's sake, don't be a bigot. One of the most colorful characters I knew in my childhood was a guy named Johnny, who was a dwarf, about 4 feet, 8 inches tall. He worked in the import/export business and often sold canned goods to my grandparents' little grocery store. He was a sunny, expansive personality, and he'd arrive in a big yellow Cadillac with a cigar in his mouth, sometimes with a 6-foot blonde on his arm.

Because the import/export business barely paid him enough to take care of his medical bills—let alone the Cadillac and the blondes—Johnny also worked as the doorman and look-out at a double-decker house where upstairs there was a "house of ill-repute" and downstairs a bookmaking joint. My father never went upstairs, but I spent a lot of time in the foyer of that house, waiting for him to come out of the bookmaker's.

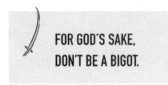

WHEN YOU ARE THE BOSS, IT'S REALLY HARD TO HIRE PEOPLE UNLIKE YOURSELF, EITHER IN PERSONALITY OR IN EXPERTISE. DO IT ANYWAY.

And Johnny was just terrific to me, one of the first adults ever to take an interest in me. He'd even treat me to the zoo now and then, and I noticed that people would just say the cruelest, most hurtful things to him because he was a dwarf. I couldn't understand it because he was such a nice guy. This gave me an early dislike of discrimination in any form—and the sense that underdogs are often worth a second look.

FOR GOD'S SAKE, DON'T BE A BIGOT.

Legal issues aside, we all know that there is a connection between bias and insecurity. If you insist on building an army of clones—and reject any candidate who doesn't fit the type—just understand that you are broadcasting your own weaknesses. Don't expect anybody to take you seriously.

ON THE OTHER HAND, IF THE CLONES ARE FUNNY . . .

That said, I've always looked for a few specific personal qualities in whatever wrapping they may be in. I've always looked for people who are serious, with a sense of humor. Humor is a sign of intelligence, and besides,

I enjoy a good laugh. I never, ever hired someone who was mirthless. I may have hired a few who were worthless, but never mirthless.

Hire for candor, too. We'll talk more about this in the next chapter, but one of the most difficult things about gaining power is that it becomes increasingly hard to find out the truth about any situation because people are increasingly eager to flatter you. Yes-men will allow you to light your career on fire without ever mentioning that your hair is smoking.

Look instead for seasoned, confident people, courageous people who will take the personal hit of telling you the truth rather than feeding you pleasant lies. If you hire only yes-men, the people above you will notice and think less of you.

I NEVER, EVER HIRED SOMEONE WHO WAS MIRTHLESS. I MAY HAVE HIRED A FEW WHO WERE WORTHLESS, BUT NEVER MIRTHLESS.

At some point as you rise, you will find that you are no longer in a position to personally make every hire in your area. The great benefit of hiring good people for your direct reports is that their abilities will radiate throughout your organization. At one point at John Hancock, we were having some legal issues, so we went out and found a top-notch general counsel. He liked working for Hancock and, as a result, was a fantastic emissary for us, attracting some very good lawyers who would never have considered working for us otherwise.

Having a reputation as somebody who not only can build a strong team but also can bring in people who can build strong teams is extraordinarily valuable.

HORSE-TRADE FOR TALENT

Once you've assembled a really great team, your rivals may well notice how good it is and try to poach key players. On the other hand, you may want to improve your team by poaching from them.

At some organizations, this horse-trading is formalized, an annual event not unlike a country livestock auction or the first-year draft in Major League Baseball. At John Hancock, for example, we used to have a retreat every year for the seven or eight top people in the company. Much of the time was spent talking about the talent lower down in the hierarchy and who could be switched where.

I used to love it. I always thought it was like a giant chess game with eight people playing.

Since nobody voluntarily gives up a top-notch person without getting something in return, there is a whole subtlety of language that goes on in this game. The executive trying to hang onto somebody might say, "She's not quite ready to move." Or, "She's tied up in a project, and it would ruin us if we had to move her now." Or, "She really loves her job and has expressed to me personally that she doesn't want to move for the next two years."

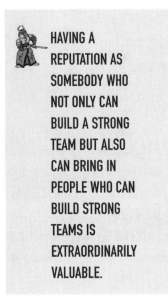

HAVING A REPUTATION AS SOMEBODY WHO NOT ONLY CAN BUILD A STRONG TEAM BUT ALSO CAN BRING IN PEOPLE WHO CAN BUILD STRONG TEAMS IS EXTRAORDINARILY VALUABLE.

And there would be a couple of us listening to this stuff, thinking, "I know that person's a star. If I could get my hands on her, I could really drive my division."

I've known lots of bosses who will publicly be lukewarm about somebody that you suspect is very bright, just to protect their resources. My advice is, if somebody interests you, read the employee's personnel files. The truth lies there. You may discover that the boss actually thinks the world of this employee and gave her the biggest raise in the division.

Meanwhile, though, other executives may be targeting your team. So you, too, may find yourself in the position of trying to give the people who work for you the accolades they deserve, while trying to protect them from being traded.

Sometimes you will just get lucky. I've had problem people a few times—people who were just a pain but who didn't quite deserve to be fired. I wouldn't *offer* to trade them, but if someone came to me and said, "Gee, I could really use Ed in my area," that was another story. I'd say coolly, "I don't know if I can give him up." Meanwhile, my heart would have leapt out of my chest in the hopes that I really did hear what I'd just heard.

At these group trading events, it's generally only the second-tier talent that is exchanged, the minor leaguers who can be spared. But there are times when the CEO will knock on your door and personally ask for somebody who is really important to your success. In such a case, you may have to be willing to give the person up. You cannot always say "No" to the CEO or president and still appear to have the organization's best interests at heart.

IF SOMEBODY INTERESTS YOU, READ THE EMPLOYEE'S PERSONNEL FILES. THE TRUTH LIES THERE.

Then, when the valued employee comes to you and asks what you think of the move, you should give him your honest assessment of it. I can remember saying to one guy, "Look, I think you're going to be working for a jerk who is not going to be helpful to you. If you stay, I'll let you out of here in a year or two, and then I guarantee that you'll go to a better boss than the one you'd get now."

Then it's up to the employee whether to stay or go.

FIRE GRACEFULLY

You will make personnel mistakes. The trick is not making too many and not failing to resolve the problem promptly when you know somebody has to go.

When I was a child, I'd often go with my grandfather and father to a meat-packing operation where they would pick up meat for our family grocery store. You had to go through the slaughterhouse to get upstairs to the cold lockers where the meat was stored. Since this was such an Italian community, veal was really in demand. And the way they slaughtered veal was by cutting the calf's throat and then hanging it up to bleed out. I'll never forget the first time I saw that. I was about four or five. Obviously, this was not Looney Tunes, and I was really upset. I said to my father in Italian, "It's terrible."

YOU CANNOT ALWAYS SAY "NO" TO THE CEO OR PRESIDENT AND STILL APPEAR TO HAVE THE ORGANIZATION'S BEST INTERESTS AT HEART.

My grandfather said wryly, "It could be worse."

"What do you mean, Dad?" my father asked my grandfather.

My grandfather nodded at me. "Tell David *he* could be a veal calf."

Having to fire people is terrible. But remember, it could be worse.

The important thing to understand about firing is that it is both an art and a science. It's a science in the sense that you have to do things by the book according to the organization's own policies and according to the law.

And it's an art in the sense that you have to accomplish this firing without causing too much of a scene. If you engender a lot of bitterness with the way you fire, it is very bad for your reputation because it is bad for your organization's reputation.

Of course, by the time you reach a firing, there may be considerable anger or desire for revenge on your side. Well, if there were ever a time to swallow such emotions and treat an event coolly, as a business transaction, a firing is it. This is no time for any kind of macho display. It is much wiser to keep the dignity of the person you are firing intact.

First, in the case of performance problems, surprises are a bad idea. Admit your mistakes early, but don't act rashly. Generally, it's better to warn an employee that she has to accomplish a set list of things in order to make it—even if that means you have to hang on to her longer than you want to, knowing full well that she won't be able to meet your conditions. This will give you time to prove the case against her, either to protect the organization legally or to help your bosses see the rationale for the firing.

How you handle the actual firing is extraordinarily important. By definition, it is a closed-door session. My advice is, make sure that you have a witness in the room, preferably an attorney who has been fully briefed in advance. First of all, the presence of a witness makes it a more dignified procedure. The simple fact that there is a third party to the conversation who can corroborate your story also makes the likelihood of a lawsuit that much less. And you'll have somebody there to protect you. If you inadvertently say something you shouldn't, it can be corrected on the spot.

> BY THE TIME YOU REACH A FIRING, THERE MAY BE CONSIDERABLE ANGER ON YOUR SIDE. WELL, IF THERE WERE EVER A TIME TO SWALLOW SUCH EMOTIONS, A FIRING IS IT.

Finally, the lawyer is likely to emerge from your office and broadcast that you handled the firing really well—which can send stock in your leadership abilities soaring.

You, on the other hand, should be extremely discreet about the entire business. Some executives are actually stupid enough to brag about what went on in a firing. It's not good to share the lascivious details because they spread through the organization like a virus. Allow your now-former employee her privacy. That way you don't provoke a lawsuit, and you don't appear to enjoy inflicting misfortune on the people who work for you.

FIRING IS NOT ALWAYS THE ANSWER

There is no question that firings are political, and they will have ramifi-cations throughout your organization. So you have to consider what are firing offenses. Incompetence, clearly. Any kind of fraud, clearly. An offense against a client, clearly. But insubordination, talking out of school, being undermining—those things are only a maybe. And sometimes you can accomplish more by *not* firing somebody who's offended you. I learned this from one of my bosses at John Hancock, who handled a dif-ficult situation in a truly classy way.

I'd recently gotten a promotion and was overseeing a sales force that was new to me when I was told by our investigators that one of my peo-ple had moved money from his client's account to his own personal account. We'll call the salesman Rick. He had used the money for six or eight months and then repaid it. In effect, Rick had borrowed from his clients without their permission. In most circles, this is called *stealing*.

I was new at my job, and I was getting a lot of pressure to let this pass because Rick was one of our top producers and had a lot of friends in the company. "Look, kid," people were saying to me, "he's an honest guy. You need to apologize to him."

So they arranged a lunch. At lunch, I asked Rick, "Did you move this money or not?"

He said, "I moved it, but I was always good for it, and the client didn't get hurt at all."

I said, "What if you'd *died* before that money had been paid back?"

He couldn't answer that question.

I pushed myself back from the table, left my lunch on the plate, and said, "I'm going back to my office. If your resignation isn't on my desk in the next half an hour, we will prosecute you."

> MAKE SURE THAT YOU HAVE A WITNESS IN THE ROOM, PREFERABLY AN ATTORNEY WHO HAS BEEN FULLY BRIEFED IN ADVANCE.

One day soon after, I was talking to another salesman, who said, "I'm really sorry to hear about your problem."

"What problem?"

"Well," he said, "I heard that you're being sued for firing somebody without cause and might get fired yourself any day." I was not being sued, and I'd never fired anybody unfairly.

I soon learned that this rumor was nonetheless running wild through the sales force. I spent a week trying to track its source. This was not unlike trying to find Typhoid Mary. Finally, I pinned it to two guys who were friends with Rick.

 **SOMETIMES YOU CAN ACCOMPLISH MORE BY NOT FIRING SOMEBODY WHO'S OFFENDED YOU.**

My boss—let's call him Frank—called for a meeting with them in his office, and they admitted everything.

"Now," Frank said to them, "what you're going to do is pick up the phone and call everybody you talked to and tell them you told them a lie. But first, you're going to walk David over to his office and you're going to apologize to him. I'm only pressing the apology because I want him to tell you whatever he wants to tell you in person."

This was very deft of Frank. He was recognizing my right to be angry and to vent or to do anything else I needed to do, short of throwing them out into the street.

We walked over to my office, and the guilty pair, as you can imagine, were both chagrined and sheepish. They started to stutter their apologies out, and I stopped them.

"Frank says you're going to stay in the company. That wouldn't be my call," I told them, "but from this moment on, I will never, ever speak to you again. Don't ever talk to me, don't ever call me, don't ever write to me. If you see me at a company meeting, you are to walk the other way."

I was with John Hancock for 13 more years and never spoke to either one of them again, even though I saw them a few times a year.

I learned a great lesson from Frank's way of dealing with those two. We could have fired them, especially since they'd admitted that they'd lied. And I was ready to pull that trigger. But Frank knew that it would probably win me a reputation for being thin-skinned.

> **THESE GUYS HAD A SCARLET LETTER PROMINENTLY PINNED TO THEIR SHIRTS. THEY BECAME LIVING EMBLEMS OF WHY NOT TO SLANDER PEOPLE.**

And he did not want to go to war with the sales force, which already found me unsympathetic. So, by showing some compassion and allowing the black sheep to stay, we eased tensions. At the same time, since I refused to have any contact with them, these guys had a scarlet letter prominently pinned to their shirts. They became living emblems of why not to slander people.

Over the years, I'd occasionally show some Frank-style mercy and allow somebody else I could have fired to stay on in a diminished capacity. The message, "Don't do what this person did," stayed fresh in people's minds far longer that way than if I'd thrown the offender into the abyss, where he would have been forgotten in a week or two.

Of course, there are pleasanter ways to motivate people than by putting their peers into the stocks. We'll talk about those in the next chapter.

WHEN IT COMES TO LAYOFFS, SOME FLEXIBILITY IS ONLY RIGHT

Generally, when people lose their jobs because the company is trying to reduce expenses, it happens in relatively large numbers. You may very well not know the full circumstances surrounding every decision made by the layers of managers underneath you.

Sometimes managers will use layoffs as a way to get rid of their lower-performing employees. However, sometimes the people laid off are absolutely terrific. If the layoff represents a particular hardship to them . . . well, they certainly didn't deserve such bad luck.

This is a situation in which it really pays to be a human being. I always had an unwritten policy that in a layoff, the extraordinary cases could come to see me. I'd have somebody from personnel or the legal department there, and they'd get a hearing.

One guy came to see me and told me that his wife had recently been diagnosed with cancer. She had no medical benefits of her own, and he couldn't afford to lose his.

He said, "Could you see your way clear to keeping me on for just a year?"

He offered to move to a different department if that would be helpful—he'd do any job—and if I wanted, he'd write his resignation letter, dated a year from then, that very day.

Of course I let him stay! For all I know, he's still with the company.

I can remember one superior who was unhappy with me for making exceptions when there were layoffs because he was afraid we were going to be sued by the people who hadn't gotten a reprieve.

So when I came across somebody who deserved a break, I just changed the person's job title and transferred them somewhere where they weren't making cuts.

He still wasn't happy. "You make an exception every time you hear a sob story," he complained.

I pointed out to him that the sob stories happened to be real.

"It's not good for the shareholders," he said.

> **IT'S IMPORTANT THAT YOUR EMPLOYEES SEE THAT YOU ARE NOT HEARTLESS.**

I didn't see it that way.

Fortunately, I soon went to work at John Hancock, where CEOs Jim Morton and Steve Brown made sure that all the managers underneath them understood that we were a company with some humanity.

If you never spare the ax, you will build a truly harsh organization, one where the people who work for you only give the minimum they can get away with because they know that's all you will give them.

It's important that your employees see that you are not heartless. They will work twice as hard for you. And on a little bit of mercy, your shareholders will probably reap considerable returns.

THE PEOPLE YOU HAVE TO MOTIVATE

You Are a Fool if You Think They Love You

*It's not what you pay a man,
but what he costs you that counts.*

Will Rogers

When I worked for the computer giant Control Data in the 1970s, the company had developed a mainframe-based software system called *PLATO* that was supposed to be the answer to all forms of education throughout the United States, from elementary schooling to management training at the highest levels.

So, if you were a manager at Control Data, you were a PLATO guinea pig. You were required to spend a certain number of hours in front of a terminal answering a series of personnel questions, such as, "If an employee comes to you and says she's pregnant and is not sure she wants to work after she has the child, what would you do?"

The machine would offer you four choices. Wow, *multiple* choices! How innovative! Management, according to Control Data, was a check-the-box problem.

Actually, management is just the opposite kind of problem. There is no mathematical matrix intricate enough to describe the challenges you will face in higher management.

You may now have thousands of people underneath you, who work in dozens of different fields. This is very different from supervising a department of 10 like-minded souls who all do similar jobs. Managing at this level is a tremendous test of your humanity, your discipline, and your ability to handle highly complex relationships.

THERE IS NO MATHEMATICAL MATRIX INTRICATE ENOUGH TO DESCRIBE THE CHALLENGES YOU WILL FACE IN HIGHER MANAGEMENT.

The absolute best management training you can have is working for good managers. Unfortunately, given the pressures of organizational life today, good managers are all too rare. So let me tell you a few things I've learned.

The good news about managing at a higher level is that many of your direct reports will now be as ambitious as you are. Ambitious people are easy to motivate. They *want* to get ahead.

The bad news is that many of them will know a lot more than you know about their own particular subjects. Since you are responsible for the success of their endeavors, you are really at their mercy.

And the truth is that you cannot afford to have any great number of people who work for you be negative about you. That is not an option. Often, in a race for the top job, it's the person who isn't a complete jerk who wins.

HEY, SMARTY PANTS—YOU ARE NOT AN EXPERT AT EVERYTHING

It's inevitable, as you rise, that you wind up managing areas of your organization that are completely unfamiliar to you. If you're a professor of chemical engineering at a university and you end up as provost, there are going to be parts of that university about which you will have no clue. The law school may be aflame over an issue that only puzzles you. In my case, marketing and communications were my areas of expertise. But as I rose, I found myself managing people who designed computer systems, made sophisticated investments, and developed complicated actuarial formulas—none of which I could do to save my life.

YOU CANNOT AFFORD TO HAVE ANY GREAT NUMBER OF PEOPLE WHO WORK FOR YOU BE NEGATIVE ABOUT YOU. THAT IS NOT AN OPTION.

Most management books will tell you that the answer to this dilemma is to hire people who are smarter than you in those areas you know little about. That's half an answer, as far as I'm concerned. Of course you do that, but it's not that simple. First of all, how do you know they're smart enough? If you know nothing about their subjects, they only have to be a little bit smarter than you to seem really smart. And how do you get these people to do what you want when you don't fully understand what they do?

You can't solve this problem by pretending, just because you are a senior player, to be expert at something you are not. But I've seen people make this very mistake many, many times. Managers become defensive or arrogant and work very hard simply to learn the vocabulary of the field. And soon the chemical engineer is lecturing somebody who has spent a career analyzing constitutional law on the subject she knows best.

THE EXPERTS IN FIELDS OUTSIDE YOUR OWN WILL INEVITABLY RESENT YOU AS A MANAGER.

I can remember, when I was doing advertising work, one of my bosses complaining about a television commercial that ended with a close-up. "Where's the top of the guy's head?" the boss asked, intensely exasperated.

"It's outside the frame," I explained. "The director is using a close-up to focus in on the guy's mood. It's a pretty common thing to do."

"I find it difficult to watch a commercial," he said stubbornly, "when I can't see the top of a guy's head."

Possibly this boss was a member of some primitive tribe that had never before seen video and so was incapable of comprehending its conventions. Possibly he was an idiot.

Nothing is worse than a boss who doesn't know what he's talking about because when he is adamant about his stupidity, you are compelled to follow his orders. Then you have to go back to your people and justify reshooting the commercial at some peculiar distance just to make sure that every last strand of the actor's hair is visible.

Behaving like that boss is the fastest possible way to lose the respect of the people who work for you. Remember, the experts in fields outside your own will inevitably resent you as a manager, one, because you're not one of them; two, because they don't understand the things you *are* expert in; and three, because they think their field is more important anyway.

What they really want, in any case, is for you to go away. But mere resentment may boil over into rage if you pretend to understand in a few weeks what they have spent half a lifetime learning.

My advice is, don't insult the experts. Get some outside help instead. Hire a consultant you trust who can help you understand whether your people are doing the right thing. Don't hit them over the head with the consultant, either. Use her discreetly, just to keep yourself informed of potential problems.

And then listen really, really carefully to your people. Defer to their expertise whenever you can. Instead of questioning them on the finer points of their business, probe the fundamentals. Ask the kinds of questions that can be posed in layman's terms: Is this going to work? Why are you so confident? What happens if it doesn't?

When I took over the investment areas at John Hancock, some of the investment people had zero respect for the experience I brought to the job—or even the fact that I had helped to win the many billions of dollars in insurance premiums and assets under management that they now invested. Some of them were under the impression that every day somebody came from Vermont with a big truck and dumped money for them on the loading dock. That was the extent of their interest in the revenue-generating side of our business.

> MERE RESENTMENT MAY BOIL OVER INTO RAGE IF YOU PRETEND TO UNDERSTAND IN A FEW WEEKS WHAT THEY HAVE SPENT HALF A LIFETIME LEARNING.

The investment people's sole objective was to earn the company money by putting those revenues out at the highest rates of return. They were even compensated differently than the rest of the company, on the degree to which they beat the average returns other companies experienced on similar investments. In other words, if they took on riskier investments that paid better, their paychecks rose.

I knew relatively little about investing, but I did know this much: When I was a kid, my father had bet compulsively on horse races, so I understood the difference between a long shot and the favorite—and the reason a winning bet on a long shot paid better. Long shots don't all pay off. So that's what I asked about.

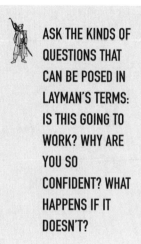

ASK THE KINDS OF QUESTIONS THAT CAN BE POSED IN LAYMAN'S TERMS: IS THIS GOING TO WORK? WHY ARE YOU SO CONFIDENT? WHAT HAPPENS IF IT DOESN'T?

For example, we were considering a big investment in a poultry farm that offered an unusually good rate of return.

I asked, "What can go wrong?"

"Nothing," somebody answered. "It's a fairly predictable investment because between cat food, fertilizer, human consumption, and consumption at the zoo, there's a great market for chicken."

I begged to differ. "This loan is not really collateralized because all you have is chicken coops, a few thousand acres of farmland in the middle of nowhere, and a pile of bird droppings to sell as fertilizer. So what happens if you have to stop killing chickens?"

They looked at me as if I were a madman.

Then a senior person asked, carefully, "Why would we stop killing chickens?"

I said, "Well, chickens get the flu. What if they all die and therefore we don't have any chickens to kill for 180 days? How much money do we lose?"

It was inconceivable to these people that this could happen, but the answer was some huge number—particularly when you figure in the fact that if you are killing chickens, there are no new eggs making new chickens. So then I asked the next question: "How much of our portfolio do we have in chickens versus our competitors?"

It turned out we had a lot more in chickens than they did because we were willing to take on more uncollateralized risks.

"I don't know your business," I said. "I'm just telling you that you have no justification here for taking on more risk than our competitors, except for the fact that you're getting paid more for it. Don't tell me we can analyze chicken farms better than the competition."

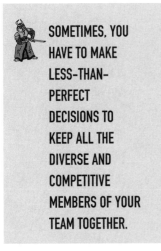

SOMETIMES, YOU HAVE TO MAKE LESS-THAN-PERFECT DECISIONS TO KEEP ALL THE DIVERSE AND COMPETITIVE MEMBERS OF YOUR TEAM TOGETHER.

My two or three questions really unsettled these people—and made it clear that even if I didn't understand the finer points of their business, I was watching their work.

Managing areas that you know relatively little about is one of the greatest challenges you'll face as you rise. When in doubt, simplify the issues, stay out of the details, and make sure your experts know that you will hold them accountable for the outcome.

MAKE SOME DECISIONS FOR THE TEAM

Of course, the challenge of managing many diverse departments and divisions is not just about ensuring good results from each of them. You also have to balance these departments against each other and give each discipline enough respect. You can easily make an enemy among your own troops just by consistently brushing off one group.

Remember, when you get to the higher levels of organizational life, most of the people around you are used to getting their own way. They're offended if their judgment is not considered. It may not be fun, spending hours listening to a lawyer's opinion on a product development question and trying to find the nugget of wisdom in there. It may seem like a waste of time. But it isn't.

You need that lawyer to help you make informed decisions, even if you don't always agree with her.

Sometimes, you even have to make less-than-perfect decisions to keep all the diverse and competitive members of your team together. For example, I have put out financial products in my career that I thought might be slightly riskier than they should be. But it was important to have a product that the marketing people felt strongly they could lead with.

On the other hand, there'd be times when the people in another discipline would convince me that we were taking on too much risk, and I wouldn't allow a product to go out with certain features. At other times, I would put out a product early, knowing full well that the technology people were right when they told me that if we waited four more months, we could produce something better and more profitable. But I did it anyway because our sales force was about to abandon us if we didn't deliver something.

As long as you don't consistently make decisions in favor of one discipline over another, you will be able to gather a strong, balanced team around you. Creating a diverse but loyal team is a way of proving to your superiors that you are not biased in favor of your own discipline and are capable of the broad outlook required for higher management. That's watched very carefully from the top of the house.

> IF IT APPEARS THAT YOU MAKE ALL YOUR DECISIONS IN ONE DIRECTION—IF THEY ARE ALWAYS MOTIVATED BY SHORT-TERM FINANCIAL GAIN, OR BY EXTREME CAUTIOUSNESS ON THE LEGAL FRONT, OR BY NIFTY TECHNOLOGY AT THE EXPENSE OF ALL ELSE—YOU WILL NOT RISE.

If it appears that you make all your decisions in one direction—if they are always motivated by short-term financial gain, or by extreme cautiousness on the legal front, or by nifty technology at the expense of all else—you will not rise. Your superiors will conclude that your point of view is too narrow for a wider role within the organization.

Sometimes, you have to compromise in ways that will not make a huge difference in your results but that will make a huge difference in your leadership.

TRUTH IS A POWERFUL MANAGEMENT TOOL

You know that you've become powerful in an organization when you overhear people talking about you in the cafeteria, and they refer to you only by your first name: "I saw David order the pizza." It's not necessarily a sign of endearment that your last name is no longer necessary, but it is definitely a sign of power.

Unfortunately, there are costs to that power. People become increasingly reluctant to bring you bad news. At the higher levels of organizational life, you spend a lot of time stretching for the truth—and if people refuse to give it, the results can be disastrous.

 IT'S NOT NECESSARILY A SIGN OF ENDEARMENT THAT YOUR LAST NAME IS NO LONGER NECESSARY, BUT IT IS DEFINITELY A SIGN OF POWER.

For example, when I was at John Hancock, we had a couple of renegade salespeople who were using our brand to sell some other company's viatical settlements. Viaticals are the life insurance equivalent of reverse mortgages: A salesperson finds old or terminally ill people holding life insurance policies who are desperate for some ready cash. He buys their insurance policies at a small percentage of their face value and then collects the full value of the policies when these frail people die. It's a product John Hancock would not sell, a predatory product that is completely inconsistent with the John Hancock brand.

But one morning I learned that a handful of our salespeople were being investigated for defrauding their viatical investors. Why hadn't the people supervising these salespeople warned me that they were selling viaticals? Because my senior employees were going to try to make it go away before I found out.

As a result, I had to learn about this problem another way—from our regulators. And so did my boss and the entire board of directors. One of your primary jobs as a senior executive is not embarrassing your boss or your board. My employees had put me in the awkward position of doing just that because I didn't know what was happening in my own area. Employees who cover up problems like this can do severe damage

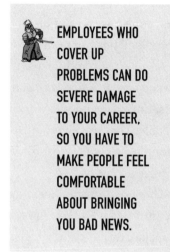

EMPLOYEES WHO COVER UP PROBLEMS CAN DO SEVERE DAMAGE TO YOUR CAREER, SO YOU HAVE TO MAKE PEOPLE FEEL COMFORTABLE ABOUT BRINGING YOU BAD NEWS.

to your career, so you have to make people feel comfortable about bringing you bad news.

The most valuable employees are those willing to rain on your parade when it's necessary—willing even to rain on a parade they organized themselves. For example, as one of Merrill Lynch's top bond executives, Jeffrey Kronthal had helped to make Merrill a leader in the market for collateralized debt obligations, complicated investment vehicles that bundle different kinds of debt and derivatives, including mortgage-backed securities.

In 2006, however, according to the *Wall Street Journal,* Kronthal began warning his bosses that the firm's exposure to the mortgage market was growing too large. Nonetheless, Merrill kept pushing its chips into mortgage-related securities, and Kronthal was replaced. Then subprime borrowers began defaulting on their loans in large numbers, and Merrill was forced to take over $20 billion in related write-downs in the last half of 2007.

Kronthal was clearly right, and in late 2007, he was rehired by Merrill. My advice is, make it clear that you value the Kronthals on your own team.

Encourage your employees to bring bad news to you individually so that they don't have to be shamed publicly for unpopular opinions or any mistakes they may have made. Encourage them to come to you even when they don't have a solution. Sometimes there is no immediate solution to a problem, but you need to know what is happening anyway.

As you begin to manage more senior people, one of the things you have to accept is that you won't spend most of your day having fun conversations. The people working for you now are very experienced and capable. They are not going to ask your advice unless there is something wrong. As a result, most of your meetings with them will be about how to solve problems.

These one-on-one meetings are where the sausage is really made in organizational life. You have to welcome them because it is very difficult to make decisions at the higher levels if you don't have all the facts.

Create an environment where your direct reports actually look forward to meeting with you, even if the subject of the meeting is going to be

ONE-ON-ONE MEETINGS ARE WHERE THE SAUSAGE IS REALLY MADE IN ORGANIZATIONAL LIFE.

unpleasant. Develop a good bedside manner so that they'll think of visiting you as not unlike a visit to the doctor when they have a terrible splinter in their toe. They are going in with some pain, the toe will become more painful before it gets better, but they know that the pain is going to be relieved.

Make it clear that the punishment for telling you bad news late—when gangrene has already set in—is far more severe than the punishment for bringing bad news early.

However, understand that you will never get the kind of candor you want from your employees unless you are honest with them, too. I used to work for a boss who would tell you exactly what he thought you needed to know and nothing more, as if we were in the CIA. He'd dole out one piece of information to one person and another piece to another person. You don't build a team that way—you build paranoia.

Other bosses spill everything only to two or three trusted favorites. Well, organizations are not elementary school playgrounds where the kid with the ball decides which other two kids get to play. There is nothing worse than working for someone who keeps secrets from you. It's insulting.

So, when something is wrong, tell all your direct reports exactly what's wrong. Why you're not going to make your quarterly numbers, why this product's failing, or why this product is selling so quickly that it's scaring you. I would bring everybody into that kind of discussion, my head of personnel, the advertising people, everybody, because they were all getting paid on that basis—on the performance of the division—so they all deserved to have enough information to help the division succeed.

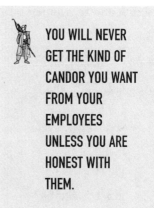

YOU WILL NEVER GET THE KIND OF CANDOR YOU WANT FROM YOUR EMPLOYEES UNLESS YOU ARE HONEST WITH THEM.

Most of your rivals will treat the people who work for them like children. You can win incredible loyalty simply by treating people like adults who can accept the truth. You will also build a team that way because your key people now all share the same information and can work together to act on it.

People want in. People want to be part of the life of the organization, whether the news is good or bad. They want to know. So let them.

REACH DOWN TO EXCISE A BLOOD CLOT

Sometimes, you won't get the truth, no matter what you do. Truth is not flowing from some area. Your directives are not being followed, sales are not going up or fund-raising is stalled, work is proceeding incredibly slowly, information is being filtered to the point of meaninglessness—and you are puzzled as to why.

Generally, there are two explanations: Either people do not have the resources they need, or you have a blood clot. A blood clot is somebody who is trying to stop your initiatives in order to undermine you, rebel against a decision you have made, or cut you out of the decision making altogether.

At the higher levels of organizational life, the blood clots generally know exactly what they are doing, and they can be really sophisticated about blocking your ideas. The trick is finding them.

Unfortunately, if you ask why work is progressing so slowly in a big staff meeting, somebody will inevitably make you a chart with lots of dots and bars on it and try to mess with your head.

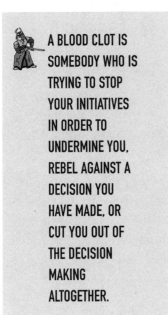

A BLOOD CLOT IS SOMEBODY WHO IS TRYING TO STOP YOUR INITIATIVES IN ORDER TO UNDERMINE YOU, REBEL AGAINST A DECISION YOU HAVE MADE, OR CUT YOU OUT OF THE DECISION MAKING ALTOGETHER.

Far better to say to a trusted aide, "Go find out the answers for real." Even more effective is to meet with the six people who actually *do* the work in question. Sometimes I would just walk down to a department where I sensed some trouble and ask the people there point-blank why they weren't getting more done. I'd cause a panic and a stir, but in all likelihood, I'd find out what was going on.

Or I'd demand that the six people producing too little and their boss come to my office. Then I'd ask the simple question, "How do you spend your day?" If the staffers were afraid to talk to me, it generally meant that their boss was intimidating them. This was a good hint that I might have a dangerous blood clot.

Reaching down like this is a good way to let the leader of a sluggish department know that she now has a red laser dot on her forehead because you are no longer buying the official story. A potential blood clot may well dissolve under such pressure.

But even this may not always work. I once had a direct report I'd brought in from outside the organization to run a large division with billions of dollars in revenue. We'll call him Sam. I was quite enamored of Sam's overall talent. He was well organized and so articulate, a fantastic presenter. His division was generally doing well, in part because the prior management of that division had done such a good job, and he was taking credit for these residual results.

IF YOU ASK WHY WORK IS PROGRESSING SO SLOWLY IN A BIG STAFF MEETING, SOMEBODY WILL INEVITABLY MAKE YOU A CHART WITH LOTS OF DOTS AND BARS ON IT AND TRY TO MESS WITH YOUR HEAD.

But I was beginning to get the sense that some of Sam's businesses were going soft. When I'd ask questions in review meetings, I'd get vague excuses, such as, "There was a one-time aberration in pricing, but things are picking up."

Now, when you rise into the highest echelon in an organization, you usually have your own staff people—finance people and technical experts—who mirror the staff people in the divisions. At that level, your people tend to be pretty sharp, like barracudas. Organizational courtesies demand that you keep the barracudas in the tank and off their divisional counterparts unless you think a division may be in trouble.

I suspected that Sam was shading the truth. So I let the barracudas out in advance of the next staff meeting to collect some hard data from Sam's people.

They came back empty-handed, but Sam then really prepared for the meeting. A lot of his people showed up, they were crisply choreographed, and the colored charts were beautiful.

And I still did not have answers to my questions.

Since I'd hired Sam and respected his talents, I continued to send warning signals over a number of months that everybody needed to know the truth and that smiley faces would not suffice.

Meanwhile, the barracudas were banging on the glass because they knew that I was being "handled." Your staff people are always smarter about this kind of thing than you are.

It turned out that Sam had decided that he would build an empire with no interference from me, and he thought the best way to do it was to keep me in the dark. So he'd ordered his people not to answer my questions or those from the barracudas. My warnings only made him tighten the lid. He and he alone would answer my questions . . . which really meant deflect them.

YOU MUST GET RID OF BLOOD CLOTS WHEN YOU FIND THEM BECAUSE THEY WILL ROB YOU OF YOUR OWN ABILITY TO SUCCEED.

In the last chapter, I said that even some really nasty behavior is not always a firing offense. But being a blood clot does not fall into this category. You must get rid of blood clots when you find them because they will rob you of your own ability to succeed. They will paint a false picture that will make it impossible for you to make balanced decisions, and balanced decisions are what you are being paid for.

Blood clots are the very reason that they invented moving companies with vans and boxes. If you find a blood clot, remember, it's possible to pack up an office in under an hour.

I not only fired Sam, but I also fired the six or seven people underneath him who'd failed to give my people the data they'd asked for. If one of my bosses earlier in my career had asked me to lie to a senior officer or stonewall him, I wouldn't have done it. But these characters were loyal only to Sam and weak in terms of their loyalty to the organization, so they had to go.

Despite the mass execution, this story has a happy ending. Suddenly people all over the organization were blurting out all kinds of things to me I'd never learned before—information that was very helpful, as well as some I didn't need.

DON'T ALLOW YOUR SUBORDINATES TO DRAG YOU ONTO THE TENNIS COURT

The problem with reaching down below your direct reports too often, even for information, is that you may give the impression that you are accessible to everybody. And the next time anybody at any level has any kind of problem, they may think that they should come to you to fix it. Then you find that you're like Jimmy Carter, deciding who plays on the White House tennis court, while the great issues of the day go unaddressed.

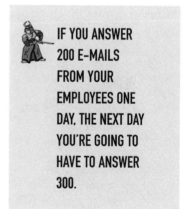

IF YOU ANSWER 200 E-MAILS FROM YOUR EMPLOYEES ONE DAY, THE NEXT DAY YOU'RE GOING TO HAVE TO ANSWER 300.

You cannot give 5,000 people unfettered access to your office. Those executives who brag that everybody in the company has their e-mail address are just absurd. That is one of the dumbest things I have ever, ever heard. If you answer 200 e-mails from your employees one day, the next day you're going to have to answer 300.

And soon people are writing to you, "My boss was unfair to me. What are you going to do about it?" The next thing you know, you are being deposed in a lawsuit, which represents even more time spent managing the tennis courts when you really ought to be dealing with issues of import.

It's a very tricky balancing act that you have to master as you rise in an organization. You can't afford to be a person in a bubble, too removed from your employees to grasp what's happening around you. At the same time, it should be clear to everyone below your direct reports that it is not okay to bother you unnecessarily. That's the message.

In higher management, you cannot leave your office door completely open. You simply have to set up some barriers.

WHAT IS THIS STRANGE RELATIONSHIP?

The most important barriers you have to set up between yourself and the people you manage are social and emotional.

This is directly counter to one of the most common workplace clichés: People who work well together are like families. If your idea of yourself as

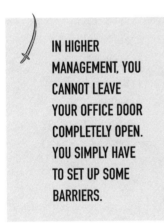

IN HIGHER MANAGEMENT, YOU CANNOT LEAVE YOUR OFFICE DOOR COMPLETELY OPEN. YOU SIMPLY HAVE TO SET UP SOME BARRIERS.

a boss is somehow to be the head of the family or the respected older brother or sister, I have one piece of advice for you: Get a life. Marry somebody; make a family of your own.

And if you are in any way like those desperate bosses Jared Sandberg wrote about in the *Wall Street Journal* who insist that their employees "friend" them on Web sites like MySpace or Facebook, you really need to find an old address book. Spend more time with your college roommates, who actually did think you were hilarious, before you had any power whatsoever.

Just admit to yourself that once you hit higher management, the people who work for you are not going to love you. They may very well not even like you. It is not in people's nature to like being told what to do. And you can't be with a boss for a few years and not resent some of the boss's habits, so it's a good bet that people resent yours.

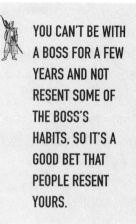

YOU CAN'T BE WITH A BOSS FOR A FEW YEARS AND NOT RESENT SOME OF THE BOSS'S HABITS, SO IT'S A GOOD BET THAT PEOPLE RESENT YOURS.

Even if they *do* like you, the relationship you have with them generally falls far short of friendship. I learned this lesson early. In my late twenties, I left a job as head of corporate communications, where I had a department of 15 people. I'd been there four years, and I thought we were all friends. I thought they liked me.

After I left, most of them would not even return a phone call. The irony was, I went back to that job a year and a half later. All the same people were there. They'd thought, "The ogre is dead. He's gone to New York, and he's not coming back." Then the ogre reappeared, and you know, they were quite nervous about not having kept in touch with me.

But who does keep in touch with their old bosses? I never did, either. If you were truly friends, well, why wouldn't you keep in touch? And the higher you go, the less likely it is that you are going to be friends. The stakes are simply too high.

So pay the people who work for you the respect of understanding why they work hard. It's not out of love for you. It is to feed their families and to get ahead.

Did the people who worked for me enjoy having to show up first thing in the morning for a meeting where I was ranting and raving about some product development thing that didn't happen, like Humphrey Bogart trying to figure out who stole his strawberries in *The Caine Mutiny*?

Probably not. They put up with it for the same reason that cavemen once went hunting barefoot in the snow. Not because they wanted to, but because they had to.

It always seemed irrelevant to me whether the people who worked for me liked me or respected me. That was their business. What I cared about was whether they did their jobs well.

That said, it is incredibly important to motivate talented people. I just don't believe that ersatz emotions like "friendship," "family love," or "organizational patriotism" *do* motivate intelligent people. We'll talk about how you win the loyalty of a brilliant team in a minute.

 PAY THE PEOPLE WHO WORK FOR YOU THE RESPECT OF UNDERSTANDING WHY THEY WORK HARD. IT'S NOT OUT OF LOVE FOR YOU. IT IS TO FEED THEIR FAMILIES.

But first, I want to say a few more words about your relationship with your coworkers. I am a big believer in being standoffish on the social front. Having an occasional group dinner with your executives is certainly appropriate, but having your social life revolve around the office is very dangerous.

The truth is that if there are 10 people on your senior management team, there's a good chance that you're going to fire three of them, and that's simply because things change. Your business faces a new challenge, and one of your managers can't rise to the occasion, so you need somebody else. And you have to be able to make that decision.

That didn't mean that I wasn't friendly with my employees in the office, but we never got together outside of business events. I didn't let our children play together. I didn't allow our lives to become entangled.

Even the business events I would keep to a minimum. For example, I actually do play golf, but nobody ever knew it. In the 35 years I was in corporate life, I never once went to a conference and picked up a golf club and played with anybody I worked with. I never wanted to spend four hours making chitchat with my boss, well aware that by the fourteenth hole, it's easy to say something stupid.

And I was no more eager to spend four hours on the golf course with my coworkers when I was the boss. The people who've played with you now feel that they're special. They go tell all their buddies, and suddenly, you appear to be playing favorites.

This is far from the only problem inherent in socializing with your employees. Some of them will use any situation outside the office, when everybody's guard is down, to lobby you for something you probably don't want to give them. Commissioned salespeople are the worst offenders on this score. They are very difficult to manage because, like bettors at a race track or in Las Vegas, they are always looking for an edge.

Even worse, social occasions give your employees the opportunity to tell you something personal that will come back to haunt you. I tried to make it clear that if people wanted to talk to me, they would have to do it in a business-like setting.

Unfortunately, I did not always succeed. A number of years ago I was in the Caribbean for a conference. I was sitting by the beach when the head of a big office wandered over to me and began telling me about a guy who worked for him whose license to sell certain products was being revoked because he was accused of committing a felony. But, the office head said, it really wasn't the guy's fault: As a child, he'd been sexually abused by his father.

HAVING AN OCCASIONAL GROUP DINNER WITH YOUR EXECUTIVES IS CERTAINLY APPROPRIATE, BUT HAVING YOUR SOCIAL LIFE REVOLVE AROUND THE OFFICE IS VERY DANGEROUS.

Trying to extricate myself, I said, "Look, I don't make up the rules about who gets to keep their license. We are a company that is somewhat forgiving, but I just don't know what the transgressions are, and I don't know the law."

I went back to the hotel and immediately reported this conversation to our auditors because it just felt funny. And it turned out that this guy himself had been accused of molesting his daughter.

We immediately got rid of him, and he soon went to jail. But I was sued anyway for wrongfully terminating his contract, and his lawyer used the fact that I had said we were a forgiving company against me. That's okay—I was more than willing to stand by that firing. But giving people access to you in a social situation can be dangerous.

SOCIAL OCCASIONS GIVE YOUR EMPLOYEES THE OPPORTUNITY TO TELL YOU SOMETHING PERSONAL THAT WILL COME BACK TO HAUNT YOU.

When you are dragged into these quasi-social business occasions, it is up to you as the boss to set the standards for behavior. I was at another convention once, earlier in my career, when I got a call at three or four in the morning. One of our salespeople had had a fight with his girlfriend and had put her head through the wall of the hotel room. I got dressed and went down to the room, where there were a couple of other executives and lawyers—and a woman sitting at the edge of the bed whose head was bleeding and covered in plaster dust.

One of the executives began saying to me, "Look, we don't have to fire him. She is not going to press charges. He's willing to go home." Then the kicker, "He's such a good salesman."

One of the lawyers then weighed in and said that I might not even have the right to fire him because the incident hadn't happened on company property.

I never should have listened to them. I wasn't mature enough yet to understand that by tolerating this behavior, I was sending a message—a very bad one—to everybody else who worked for me.

Sure enough, this guy was soon involved in another violent incident. Letting him off the first time was a huge mistake. I never made that mistake again.

Of course, you can be as careful as I was about your social exposure and still be dragged into something embarrassing simply by bumping into somebody in the hallway. The sobbing secretary I told you about in an earlier chapter certainly proves that.

Try to remember that your office is not *The Jerry Springer Show*. Hand those employees who mistake you for a priest or a psychiatrist the Kleenex—and send them as fast as you can to the legal department or personnel. Those people are the experts. If there is something you really need to know, they will tell you.

Do everything possible to discourage your employees from pouring their hearts out to you. You cannot afford to hear the details.

This may sound callous or paranoid, but getting caught up in the personal affairs of the people who work for you represents an incredible burden in terms of time. It also represents an incredible risk in terms of litigation and an incredible embarrassment in terms of your own career—because you now have to inform your boss of the seamy things happening in your division on your watch.

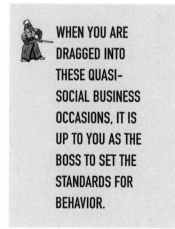

WHEN YOU ARE DRAGGED INTO THESE QUASI-SOCIAL BUSINESS OCCASIONS, IT IS UP TO YOU AS THE BOSS TO SET THE STANDARDS FOR BEHAVIOR.

This does not mean, however, that you should close your eyes and ears completely. Knowing in general terms what's happening in people's lives is part of the boss's job. You have to respect their privacy—but *I* never respected an executive who didn't know whether or not his employees had children. You have to be familiar with the broad strokes of your employees' stories in order to do the one thing that really does motivate talented people—give them what they want and need.

LOYALTY IS ABOUT GRATITUDE, NOT PATRIOTISM

You can get people to work very, very hard because they are proud of your organization or because they want your organization's prestigious name on their résumé. But relying on a blind salute to the logo to motivate people will get you just about as far as relying on their love for you.

In my experience, you build loyalty by helping each member of your team, individually, get where they want to go.

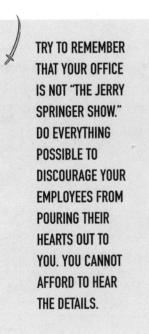

TRY TO REMEMBER THAT YOUR OFFICE IS NOT "THE JERRY SPRINGER SHOW." DO EVERYTHING POSSIBLE TO DISCOURAGE YOUR EMPLOYEES FROM POURING THEIR HEARTS OUT TO YOU. YOU CANNOT AFFORD TO HEAR THE DETAILS.

For example, say you have an employee who is 62 and thinking of taking his pension and leaving you. However, you really need his fealty and his work for another two years. It is very helpful to know that what he really wants is to buy an 80-foot boat and move to Florida in his retirement. He's been assembling the pieces, but he's just short of being able to do that. He doesn't want the 40-foot boat; he wants the 80-foot boat.

Take the trouble to learn something like that, and you can say, "Look Joe, stay, and I guarantee that you'll be able to buy that 80-foot boat. I'll bonus you, or option you, or enhance your pension, whatever it takes so that you'll never have to think about it. But I need two more years." And you will probably get them.

At the same time, on the same project, you might have a 28-year-old woman who's an IT genius. She wants to move to California because that's where her fiancé lives, but you need her.

Her fiancé is a lawyer, so you ask, "Is he any good?" And she, of course, says he's brilliant.

"I'll tell you what," you might say, "we'll bring him here and set up interviews with three law firms that work for us. I'll put in a good word. If he gets a job, we'll make sure it pays better than the one he has now." And you get her to agree to the two years you need.

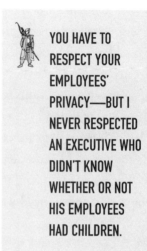

YOU HAVE TO RESPECT YOUR EMPLOYEES' PRIVACY—BUT I NEVER RESPECTED AN EXECUTIVE WHO DIDN'T KNOW WHETHER OR NOT HIS EMPLOYEES HAD CHILDREN.

The same project may also require a 37-year-old marketing person who has three small kids and is debating whether she shouldn't just stay at home. If you need her, you might make this deal: "You don't have to come to work until Monday at noon, and I'll give you Fridays off. Just promise me the two years in return."

These are not Kumbaya moments. They are far more effective. You are winning people's loyalty in action. You are not intruding on their lives; you are making a deal that recognizes that they do have lives separate from the office.

BUILD LOYALTY BY HELPING EACH MEMBER OF YOUR TEAM, INDIVIDUALLY, GET WHERE THEY WANT TO GO.

Sometimes what people need most is respect for the fact that they have personal lives. Once I had an older guy who worked for me whose son died in a car accident. The boy was only 18 or 19, and my employee and his wife were just shattered. The wake was on a Monday night in California. I had to be on the East Coast all day because of a board meeting, but I got on a late afternoon flight and, because of the time difference, made it into the wake at 8:30 at night to pay my respects. Then I flew the red-eye back.

My employee never forgot that. And when the company was having some problems and I really needed him, he was a champ for me, absolutely remarkable.

I've used my connections to help my employees' families with medical problems and with legal problems. In my experience, this builds the kind of indelible loyalty you cannot build just by having beers with your team after a long day. A chit system beats networking every time. Use your power to lend people a hand in tough times, and they will use their power to help you when you need it, too.

SOMETIMES, WHAT PEOPLE NEED MOST IS RESPECT FOR THE FACT THAT THEY HAVE PERSONAL LIVES.

The fact is, if you are going to rise high, you can expect tough times. As a country, we tend to root for the underdog and take delight in tearing the powerful apart. In the last chapter I mentioned former Disney Chairman Michael Eisner, an executive I really admired. He took a moribund children's entertainment company and turned it into a media powerhouse with a stable of remarkable brands and an amazing string of hits to its credit. Then the stock price weakened early in this decade, and a group of dissident board members led by Roy Disney, Walt's nephew, tried to oust Eisner.

My first thought was that Roy Disney should go join the seven dwarfs in the forest.

Yet I noticed something. Eisner was a brilliant executive who'd made many careers, and many of his key employees had gone on to run other organizations. He'd clearly given remarkable opportunities to the people who worked for him. But very few of them were willing to defend him when he was being attacked.

In his 2005 book, *Disney War*, author James B. Stewart points out that when the company attempted to generate letters of support for Eisner in the middle of this campaign, "the silence was deafening." At the critical 2004 annual meeting that effectively put an end to Eisner's reign, it was not just 43 percent of the Disney shareholders who withheld their votes for Eisner's reelection to the board—but, according to Stewart, 72.5 percent of Disney's own employees, voting through their 401(k)s.

Apparently Eisner, who was famous for feuding with his lieutenants, had failed to build much loyalty among the troops.

A CHIT SYSTEM BEATS NETWORKING EVERY TIME.

Well, when things are going well, you really don't need loyalty. The stock is rising or the fund-raising is ahead of schedule, everyone is getting a nice bonus, so everyone is happy. It's when things are hard that you need it. My advice is, treat the people who work for you with respect and start building that loyalty today.

OUTSIDERS WITH INFLUENCE

Be Wary, Be Right, and Be Prepared to Prove It

*You can observe a lot
by just watching.*

Yogi Berra

As difficult as it can be to manage a relationship with the people you see every day, it's that much more difficult to manage a relationship with the people you don't. You generally don't know your outside directors, clients, donors, or vendors very well— let alone the boss's friends and acquaintances. They don't know you well, either. Yet these are outsiders with influence, and they may have veto power over your rise. So you'd better handle them carefully.

Let's start with the most obviously powerful of these strangers, the people who send the money that keeps your organization rolling along.

CLIENTS AND DONORS: You Can't Avoid the Witch's House

A lot of people rise in the ranks without ever having had to confront those peculiar people who ship gold to an organization, the clients and the donors. If you've come up from the financial side, for example, you may never have dealt with them at all.

At some point on your way to the top, though, you will probably wind up in a revenue-generating role, where you will be overseeing people who are handling clients and donors. Just because you are a senior person who is not meeting with the givers of gold every day does not mean you can afford to ignore them. Your job is not just to win new revenues, but also to retain the revenues the organization has already won and, if possible, increase the amount of money existing clients or donors will send you.

JUST BECAUSE YOU ARE A SENIOR PERSON WHO IS NOT MEETING WITH THE GIVERS OF GOLD EVERY DAY DOES NOT MEAN YOU CAN AFFORD TO IGNORE THEM.

Even when you reach senior management, if you have a fragile relationship with a major donor or client, it doesn't take much for that person to affect your career. If you don't believe me, just go ahead and lose a $60 million account or a $100 million account. Lose a couple of them, and see what happens.

I learned about the power of clients as a kid of seven or eight. There was an old Italian lady who used to come into my family's grocery store. She always wore black. She lived in a dark little green house with lots of trees in the overgrown yard. She bought a lot of herbs, and the older kids were convinced that she was brewing up potions with them. They used to talk about her as a witch, and I was scared of her.

One day she called and said she wanted some groceries delivered. My mother couldn't leave the store, so the lady said, "Well, I saw David there this morning. Have him bring them."

I refused. "I won't go there," I said. I wasn't deliberately defying my parents; I literally was too afraid to go to her house.

Although I couldn't imagine that my parents would punish me for not wanting to bring groceries to the witch, they were so upset that they grounded me. It was the first time I realized the power of someone who gives a business money, even in that kind of rudimentary fashion.

That was good training. Clients and donors can be quite unpredictable and frightening. They bring the gold, so they don't have to adhere to any rules of civilized society. And they are dangerous because they have access.

 CLIENTS AND DONORS CAN BE QUITE UNPREDICTABLE AND FRIGHTENING. THEY BRING THE GOLD, SO THEY DON'T HAVE TO ADHERE TO ANY RULES OF CIVILIZED SOCIETY.

Remember, the long-standing clients or contributors in an organization often know your bosses. They may be assigned to your world now, but it's possible that your boss used to take care of their account, or has gone to their conventions as a guest, or belongs to the same country club they do.

Even if they haven't been around long, given the level of competition in this global economy, any client who spends millions of dollars with your organization has a good chance of seeing the CEO whenever she wants. I'd bet that Henry Ford never felt like he had to meet with a lot of his buyers.

But today, when somebody from a large international car-rental company asks the CEO *du jour* of Ford Motors for a meeting, chances are good she will get it.

WHEN A CLIENT'S UNHAPPY, IT'S A BIT LIKE THE RUNNING OF THE BULLS—AND YOU'RE WEARING WHITE WITH A RED SCARF WRAPPED AROUND YOUR WAIST.

Clients are more than happy to flex their muscles this way—and not only to get a better price or a better product from you, but also to play politically within your organization. Of course, big donors to nonprofits have always tried to influence the way the hospital is run, or the college football team is coached, or the art museum arranges its exhibitions. Thanks in part to all the business media that have sprung into being in the last decade, the bringers of gold in businesses are becoming just as forthright and dangerous.

They now have lots more information than they used to about what's happening inside your business. And if they are not happy with you, it can get really personal. If the client or donor, for example, hears that you're up for a promotion, he is not necessarily shy about calling up a board member and saying, "I hope you're not thinking of making this guy president."

When a client's unhappy, it's a bit like the running of the bulls—and you're wearing white with a red scarf wrapped around your waist. You may well get skewered.

CLIENTS, LIKE BABIES, NEED ATTENTION

So here's how to keep the bringers of gold happy as a senior person who is not meeting with them every day.

You have to layer your clients and donors and concentrate on the important ones. Is their importance measured by the size of the checks they send, by how long they've been sending those checks and what are their relationships with the people above you like? If the answers to those questions are big, a long time, and very tight, they need to be coddled by your team.

They shouldn't expect that they're going to be able to see you for everything. But you still have to pay attention. In the advertising business, they taught us that you have to make every client feel that he is your only client. That's good advice. If an important client is going to be in the building, drop in at the meeting, even if you are not expected. It's a show of respect. Call him every now and then to see how things are going. Make sure your people understand that if there is any hint of a problem, you're to know about it. And if there *is* a serious problem, be prepared to get on a plane in order to soothe the savage beast.

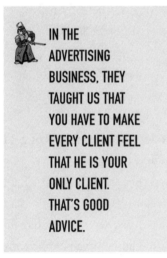

IN THE ADVERTISING BUSINESS, THEY TAUGHT US THAT YOU HAVE TO MAKE EVERY CLIENT FEEL THAT HE IS YOUR ONLY CLIENT. THAT'S GOOD ADVICE.

The second thing you have to do to keep important clients happy is be accessible at the drop of a hat. If the client really counts, make sure that she has your home phone number—not just your cell phone, but your home phone. Say to that client, "If there's a problem, call me any time."

I've had disasters happen more than once on a Friday. Inventory wasn't delivered, a television commercial was deemed horrible, or payments for group insurance were not deducted on time. Whatever the problem, the result was chaos at the clients' offices. The only thing that kept those disasters from becoming catastrophes was the fact that the clients had my home phone number.

Otherwise, those angry clients only would have gotten angrier because they would have had the whole weekend to stew about it. By Monday morning, they would no longer have cared about anything I had to say. They would have picked up the phone to call my boss.

When a client is angry, try to keep the problem off the boss's desk, but make sure you keep the boss in the loop. You can't trust that your client won't make that Monday morning phone call anyway. A sophisticated boss understands that things go wrong but doesn't like being kept in the dark and possibly seeming out of touch if the client does call. The fact that you're taking care of the problem on your own—and on a weekend—but keeping him informed about it is all to your credit.

 **WHEN A CLIENT IS ANGRY, TRY TO KEEP THE PROBLEM OFF THE BOSS'S DESK, BUT MAKE SURE YOU KEEP THE BOSS IN THE LOOP.**

The third way to keep clients happy is to serve as a *consigliere* to them. They may be spending $5 million or $20 million or $50 million with your organization. Part of the transaction is that they get your time and advice in return.

For example, maybe your client hates her bosses and is considering changing her career. Let's call her Emily. Naturally, Emily can't talk to many people inside her own organization about it.

By all means, take her to dinner. It's been several years since I left John Hancock, and I still have former clients who call me and say, "You know, I'm having a problem with my career. Can you help me think this through?"

On the other hand, never discuss your organization's internal issues with a client, ever, ever, ever! If the client turns on you, it can be used against you.

If you have a chance to meet Emily's boss, try to say something nice about her without its sounding calculating.

If Emily puts herself in the running for a job with another organization, she will probably need a reference from somebody who is going to be discreet. This is an interesting dilemma. Do you provide that reference or not?

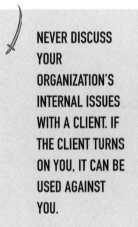

NEVER DISCUSS YOUR ORGANIZATION'S INTERNAL ISSUES WITH A CLIENT. IF THE CLIENT TURNS ON YOU, IT CAN BE USED AGAINST YOU.

On the one hand, if she gets the job, you could lose your point of entry to a major client. On the other hand, if your people have done their work well, the organization will probably keep you on anyway. And you may very well wind up getting business from a new client, once the grateful Emily moves to the new organization.

If you offer your clients good advice and help their careers along, they will come to trust you not only as a businessperson, but also as a person. And when something gets screwed up—as it inevitably will—or a new opportunity arises, that trust may make all the difference.

The fourth way to keep clients happy is to help them solve problems, not just in their businesses and careers, but also in their lives. This is not so different from motivating key employees: Treat them as human beings, and use your influence to help them. Tell your senior staff that if there's something serious going on with one of the clients—a kid gets hurt, somebody dies, or somebody's sick—you want to know in order to lend a hand.

It's particularly important to do personal favors if you are like me and are utterly unwilling to waste a nice afternoon playing golf with a client. So get the chit system rolling.

I once had a client who, when I asked how he was, replied, "Not too great. My daughter spent the weekend in her room crying." His daughter had just gotten rejection letters from a handful of private high schools in Los Angeles. She was a smart kid, but admission was very competitive, and she wound up only getting into her third choice. She knew absolutely no one going to this school.

I'd met the girl a few times at conferences, so I asked if the client and his wife would mind if I sent her a note about something that had happened to me as a kid.

"I know it's hard to listen to adults when you're 13," I wrote her. "But take that into consideration when I tell you this story. When I was 13, I really wanted to get into this one particular school, too. I had good grades, and all my best friends were going there, but I didn't get in. I ended up going to this other school, which I hated for the first semester, really hated.

"But it turns out that I met a great teacher there and some new friends who gave me an entirely new perspective and a new direction, which caused me to go to a different college and have a different career. If I had to do it all over again, I would go to the school my friends went to. But it turned out better for me that I didn't. I think you'll find that there's a reason you're going to the school you are going to. You don't know it yet, but someday you will."

Now, her parents, of course, had been telling her the same thing for a week. But the next time I saw the client, he said to me, "I can't tell you what a difference that letter made." Then he added, "I can't believe you took the time." It didn't take a lot of time—it took 20 minutes—but the client never forgot it.

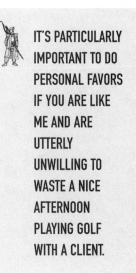

IT'S PARTICULARLY IMPORTANT TO DO PERSONAL FAVORS IF YOU ARE LIKE ME AND ARE UTTERLY UNWILLING TO WASTE A NICE AFTERNOON PLAYING GOLF WITH A CLIENT.

I had another client whose sister's lifelong dream was to run in the Boston Marathon. In general, you have to qualify for the Boston Marathon, based on your time and age, and the client's sister would never have made it. But the Marathon does reserve a few spots for more ordinary athletes. I called him back a couple of days later and said, "A preapproved application for your sister is in the mail. She just has to fill it out and send it in."

Half a year later, we had some trouble on that account, and it was a contentious problem that took months to fix. I'm convinced that we were granted the time and the opportunity to fix the problem because the client remembered this personal favor.

Now, I am not recommending that you send cards on clients' birthdays or embarrass them with elaborate gifts that they might have to return. That kind of stuff is just obvious and craven.

Just do the things that will win you a reputation as a problem solver, for problems of all kinds. That way, if something goes wrong, the client is inclined to call you rather than your bosses.

JUST DO THE THINGS THAT WILL WIN YOU A REPUTATION AS A PROBLEM SOLVER, FOR PROBLEMS OF ALL KINDS.

Again, doing favors for your customers and donors is not the same as having strong social ties to them, which I do not recommend. I would go out of my way not to have the families get involved in a client relationship because your chances of having a problem spill over into your business go way up. I had a senior sales executive, for example, whose son was dating a client's daughter. The son broke the relationship off and was not nice to the girl at all, and her parents were quite upset. How insane was that? I would *lock* my children in a room if one of them tried to date the child of one of my clients.

The final way to keep big clients happy is never to lie to them. If your company has screwed something up, tell them you screwed it up.

If the client is happy, she isn't necessarily going to express that happiness to your boss. As a CEO, if I were having dinner with a client, and she were to say, "Your guy Ed has been really terrific with us," I would know that Ed had put her up to it. A blanket endorsement is not a natural conversation at this level.

The smart move is to ask the client to say something concrete about you—for example, that you've been very sensitive to certain particular issues that the boss thinks are a weakness for you—and only if the boss asks about you.

IF YOU ARE GOING TO DEFY A CLIENT, BE RIGHT

Of course, these rules for keeping big clients happy do not mean that you should do everything a client wants. What the client wants may be detrimental to your organization.

In the insurance business, for example, underpricing is a constant temptation because you can collect the premium dollars immediately and may not have to pay any particular claim for decades, if ever. So who cares if the product is priced too low today? Institutionalize this attitude, however, and you wind up sinking the business over the long term.

At John Hancock, we had some group insurance clients we weren't making any money on. And I decided to raise their prices. They were just furious, so furious that they decided to join forces to go over my head, meet with the president of the company, and try to jam the pricing.

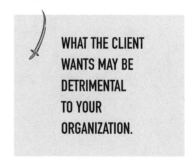

WHAT THE CLIENT WANTS MAY BE DETRIMENTAL TO YOUR ORGANIZATION.

The danger here is that the boss has to listen to these clients, and you are not in the room. Half-truths can turn into serious accusations in such a situation, such as, "Not only did David raise our premiums, but he also didn't return my phone calls for a week."

Making matters worse, another large insurance company soon decided that it wanted this set of clients, so it lowered its prices to steal them from us.

I was raked over the coals for chasing away this group of customers until I proved that we were actually losing money on these people, and did we really want them anyway?

If you are going to clash with a customer, you'd better, one, be right, and two, be prepared to defend your position.

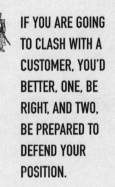

IF YOU ARE GOING TO CLASH WITH A CUSTOMER, YOU'D BETTER, ONE, BE RIGHT, AND TWO, BE PREPARED TO DEFEND YOUR POSITION.

Warn your bosses if you and a customer are having a disagreement so that when they get that first phone call, they've been somewhat inoculated. It's far worse to be blindsided by a customer willing to go above your head without discussing it with you and a boss who doesn't bother to get your point of view.

Understand also that it's not just bad client service that will keep you from being promoted, but also client service that is too good, because in that case the boss may become unwilling to move you.

LET YOUR BOSSES KNOW STRAIGHT OUT THAT IF THEY DON'T PROMOTE YOU AT SOME POINT, YOU WILL WALK. AND POSSIBLY MUCH OF THE GOLD WILL WALK WITH YOU.

I've seen it happen a thousand times. People become trapped because they are so adept at keeping the gold rolling in.

The answer to this is really simple. First, cultivate people underneath you who can help the organization keep the gold after you rise. Second, let your bosses know straight out that if they don't promote you at some point, you will walk. And possibly much of the gold will walk with you.

Scaring your bosses on this subject is not a bad idea at all.

VENDORS, THE COUNTERINTUITIVE POWER

In your relationship with clients, they have an obvious superiority. They are giving you gold. On the other hand, with vendors, you're the one passing out gold to them. When you become a decision maker who can affect the way millions of dollars are spent on printing, or consulting services, or plant care, you become a very powerful person—perhaps more powerful on the outside than you are on the inside.

So you would think that you would have control over your relationships with vendors. Well, think again. Vendors are not your friends, and often they are dangerous enemies.

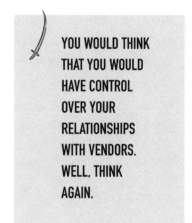

Their power arises from the close relationship they may have with your bosses. Generally, the CEO of a $10 billion company and the head of a $10 million law firm are in the same social stratum. They may be neighbors. They may play squash together. They may serve on boards together. Or they may have worked together from the time that the CEO held your job. And if you try to cut that lawyer's business, you may well hear about it from the CEO.

YOU WOULD THINK THAT YOU WOULD HAVE CONTROL OVER YOUR RELATIONSHIPS WITH VENDORS. WELL, THINK AGAIN.

Let's talk, first, about existing vendors whose livelihood suddenly becomes a line item on your budget and then about would-be vendors trying to lobby their way in.

TREAD CAREFULLY WITH THE EXTENDED FAMILY

It's stupid to dislike an existing vendor simply because he or she has been around awhile. If, however, you suspect that you are not getting good value out of the vendor, and the vendor is in a commodity business, you are probably standing on solid ground. For example, at some point in my career, the divisions I was overseeing needed a lot of printing. There was a printing company we had a long relationship with. Let's call the owner Kevin. He knew the big bosses well and had been doing everything for us for a dozen years.

The thing about printing, though, is that you can reject the product if it's no good. So quality is not the deciding factor—price is. I decided to put our printing work out for bids for the first time.

Kevin was outraged and instantly went to the two big bosses to ask how we could even question the relationship, especially since he hadn't raised his prices in three years.

"This isn't about the relationship," I said to the powers that be. "Actually, Kevin's company is excellent, one of the best around. But there are other good printers, and we have never bid out the contract, even though it's millions of dollars of company money every year."

IT'S STUPID TO DISLIKE AN EXISTING VENDOR SIMPLY BECAUSE HE OR SHE HAS BEEN AROUND AWHILE.

When it comes to price-driven contracts, the top of the house will always let you bid them out because they're afraid of being accused of favoritism.

Now that there was an open competition, Kevin lowered his rates and still came out the highest by far! What had happened over the years was that he had goosed up his prices and goosed up his prices and stopped only when he was making a fortune. Meanwhile, inside the house, it had always been taken for granted that Kevin was untouchable.

Well, we hired somebody else, and when we next bid out the contract, Kevin was again too expensive. Eventually, he stopped socializing with the bosses and ceased to be a problem.

Commodities peddlers like Kevin are much easier to handle than what I would call the subjective vendors—the accountants, the lawyers, the IT or management consultants, the investment bankers—from whom your organization is buying brainpower and lots of other difficult-to-quantify talents.

Nonetheless, you may find yourself wondering why it is that your organization uses one particular consulting firm when there are dozens of consulting firms in town that could do the work. Why are they sacred? Treated like extended family?

Generally, there is a reason. Here is an example: When I was in the advertising agency business, the CEO's son was arrested for a DUI. The CEO got a call in the middle of the night and, in turn, called the only lawyer he happened to know, his corporate lawyer. So the lawyer roused the right partner, who went to New Jersey and bailed the kid out. The partner handled the case so well that the kid got off with just a slap on the wrist, and no whisper of the story ever appeared in the papers.

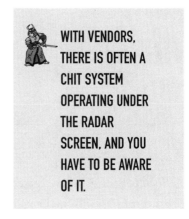

WITH VENDORS, THERE IS OFTEN A CHIT SYSTEM OPERATING UNDER THE RADAR SCREEN, AND YOU HAVE TO BE AWARE OF IT.

After that, the CEO paid full price to that firm for all the agency's legal work for years. It's very hard to dislodge a vendor who does something like that—for example, a vendor who uses his connections to get a child into the right college or uses his seat on a hospital board to get an ailing parent to the right doctors.

With vendors, there is often a chit system operating under the radar screen, and you have to be aware of it. It has nothing to do with graft or bribery. It doesn't mean that the vendor is not doing fine work, either. It's just that a personal favor was done someplace along the line that was so vital to your boss or your boss's boss that it transcends all other considerations.

If you're connected at all in your organization, you will probably be able to find out what the favor was, but you may not want to, lest the answer embarrass the people at the top. In any case, if you have a sense that there's an important chit sitting around somewhere, don't get a case of the stupids and mess with the vendor for the sake of messing with him.

SHARKS AFTER CHUM

Now let's talk about vendors who are not already ensconced in your area but are lobbying for your business through your bosses.

Your bosses are generally far away from purchasing decisions at this level, and most will claim that they don't want to be involved. But their psychology is quite interesting. Most of the top executives I know miss being hands-on. They miss being able to see immediate change. So, when a very smooth, smart lawyer, advertising executive, or software consultant says to a CEO, "Pete, we can save you $5 million if you consolidate your business with us," the CEO finds it very tempting to interfere.

EXPECT TO BE SIDESWIPED BY VENDORS ALL THE TIME.

So expect to be sideswiped by vendors all the time. And the bigger your organization is and the broader your responsibilities are, the more often this is going to happen.

If you decide that you don't want a particular vendor favored by one of the big bosses, presumably you have a legitimate reason: They're too expensive, or they don't have the right expertise. Understand, however, that whatever your reason is, it will not make this vendor cease pounding away at your bosses.

If your reason is simply that you want to own your own territory, you may well wind up resisting something that's smart just to be territorial. I've seen ambitious people make this mistake many times. They hold the fact that a vendor is connected against them when the vendor is very good and might actually help their careers.

If you are truly picking a vendor without help—maybe even in defiance of a big boss's wishes—understand that you own that vendor. If the law firm you choose loses a big case that costs the company $50 million, that is your law firm, lock, stock, and barrel. Its screw-up is your screw-up.

Expect the lawyer you've rejected, the one with social ties to your bosses, to pounce on any such screw-up and use it to raise doubts about you. Vendors are great rumor mongers in part because they're not accountable to anybody. Your ability to resist them diminishes greatly in the wake of a mistake. You can wind up having the entire responsibility in question stripped away from you.

> IF YOU ARE TRULY PICKING A VENDOR WITHOUT HELP—MAYBE EVEN IN DEFIANCE OF A BIG BOSS'S WISHES—UNDERSTAND THAT YOU OWN THAT VENDOR. ITS SCREW-UP IS YOUR SCREW-UP.

And understand that vendors can influence the course of your career over the long term. For example, if the CEO's about to retire and a vendor thinks that you have a shot at that job and you've been particularly good to him, he will say nice things about you. The opposite is true as well: If you tried to jack his firm out of there at some point, he will do everything he can to promote a rival who seems more likely to give him business in the future. None of them is suicidal, you know.

So how do you take control of these slippery relationships? My advice is to spread your business around whenever possible. If they are qualified, give all the vendors with access above you a portion of your business.

> SPREAD YOUR BUSINESS AROUND WHENEVER POSSIBLE.

Dividing up the work among specialists often makes sound business sense. I have never seen a single law firm that is equally good at everything.

At the same time, I have never seen a vendor who is satisfied with less than 100 percent of an organization's business. Each one wants every scrap, and they don't want their competitors in the company. So give each vendor some business as a tease, and keep them all hoping that they may win more down the road . . . as long as they don't tick you off. Offer them a reason to work for, not against you.

FIGHT THE BRIGHT IDEAS OF SALESPEOPLE

The worst would-be vendors are not the ones who simply lobby your boss for business, but the ones who go so far as to contribute business ideas, which you then have to fend off. For example, there was once a broker who wanted John Hancock to partner with him on a high-commission, high-risk business where we would underwrite large life insurance policies for Americans overseas, based on foreign physicals.

> **GIVE EACH VENDOR SOME BUSINESS AS A TEASE, AND KEEP THEM ALL HOPING THAT THEY MAY WIN MORE DOWN THE ROAD . . . AS LONG AS THEY DON'T TICK YOU OFF.**

Our actuaries didn't like the idea, and neither did I. When we took on big risks at John Hancock, we wanted to know who the doctors were.

Suddenly, however, my boss was simply hammering me as to why we were not in this business. I couldn't figure out the source of my miseries at first, and there is nothing worse than trying to defend yourself against a ghost. Then I realized that the broker in question belonged to a fancy golf club my boss wanted to play at. So they were golfing together.

Your tendency in a situation like this is to slough off the boss's suggestion: I've already looked at that idea and made my decision. I'm not going to deign to consider that subject again.

That is exactly the wrong way to handle this kind of outside pressure. It may be silly, and it may be time-consuming, but take the time to prove methodically why the idea does not work. Launch a study, do the research, and lay the question to rest with the facts.

THE WORST WOULD-BE VENDORS ARE THE ONES WHO GO SO FAR AS TO CONTRIBUTE BUSINESS IDEAS, WHICH YOU THEN HAVE TO FEND OFF.

That way, you accomplish a number of things. You respond respectfully to the boss. You also destroy the credibility of the golf partner who brought this idea forward. He can never plant another notion with that boss again because you have proven that he is not trustworthy.

Beware of the sin of arrogance in such circumstances. It is not enough to be right. You have to prove you're right.

MAKE SURE YOUR OUTSIDE BOARD MEMBERS SEE MORE OF YOU THAN JUST YOUR POWERPOINTS

Particularly susceptible to this kind of lobbying are your outside directors, and you are probably dealing with more of those than ever. Thanks to the business scandals of recent years, the ideal board is now an independent board made up of the fewest possible insiders. This is true even at nonprofits and universities.

By definition, these people are visitors to your world. Even the best of them won't spend more than six weeks a year at your organization, about the same amount of time that you spend on vacation.

They are simply not around enough to distinguish bad ideas from good ideas, so they are easy marks for an aggressive sales pitch by an outsider. Because you generally don't have much of a relationship with them beyond the board room, it is doubly important not to arrogantly dismiss their ideas.

These people have a lot to say about your career—more than ever, in fact, given the degree to which they are taking their oversight responsibilities seriously in this post-Enron era. But even if you are the head of a very large division, they probably only see you when you are presenting to them.

Still, board members hear things and talk among themselves. And based on very little evidence, evidence that you may never have a chance to respond to, they make judgments about you. On the day when the CEO goes to the board and says he wants to promote you, if a couple of the directors raise their hands and say, "You know, I'm not so sure," you are probably a dead man.

This is not about majority rule. It's about noise—positive or negative noise. And if the noise is negative, even the CEO may think, "I don't want to make this fight."

As a result, outside directors are a great exception to my bias against networking. I'm all for being aloof socially from those people you see all the time. However, you are running a serious risk if you remain unknown to your outside board members.

BEWARE OF THE SIN OF ARROGANCE. IT IS NOT ENOUGH TO BE RIGHT. YOU HAVE TO PROVE YOU'RE RIGHT.

You don't need to bond with them; you just need to let them learn more about you and your capabilities than they could glean in a conference room, so that the next time they hear some rumor about you or a salesman criticizes the way you are running your business, they will give you the benefit of the doubt. The trick is finding a way to interact with them without obviously campaigning for a promotion and without threatening your boss.

You might even consider going to the boss and saying, "I'm worried about the three or four directors who do not know me." She may help you get to know them.

If a couple of directors are already friendly toward you, enlist their help. Have them sponsor a dinner that will allow you to become better acquainted with the directors you don't know.

Or engineer a relationship yourself. Sometimes there are committees within an organization that include both board members and nonboard members. It is very smart to get yourself on one of those. It's also smart to get to know the people in your organization who arrange the meetings and conferences. Then, if you're going to a conference and an outside director is invited, ask those people for a favor—to be seated next to the director.

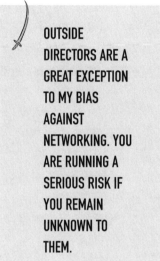

OUTSIDE DIRECTORS ARE A GREAT EXCEPTION TO MY BIAS AGAINST NETWORKING. YOU ARE RUNNING A SERIOUS RISK IF YOU REMAIN UNKNOWN TO THEM.

The CEO generally won't look askance at a move like this because often the CEO doesn't *want* to sit next to her board members. She sees—and hears—enough of them as it is.

And your rivals? The good news is that most of them will simply be too dumb to think along these lines.

UNDERSTAND THE POWER OF HAPPENSTANCE, AND BE WARY

Everywhere you go, there is a chance that you will run into somebody who has some influence with the powers that be in your organization. Here is an example: I had a guy working for me who was a perfectly sane, normal person as far as I could see, and I thought highly of his abilities. Let's call him Tony. Then one day I was talking to a friend of mine who happened to live in the same town as Tony. He asked, "Does Tony work for you?"

I said, "Yeah, he's a good guy."

My friend begged to differ. "Let me tell you something. You should see him at his son's Little League games. He is a maniac, screaming at the kids to the point where the umpires threw him off the field a few weeks ago."

Was I really going to promote somebody who screamed at little kids at a Little League game? It gave me pause.

You have to be aware that six degrees of separation is often three or four too many when it comes to organizational life. Random strangers to you are not always strangers to the people who hold your career in their hands. So it is smart to conduct yourself, in public at least, as if there is always somebody in the audience who matters.

THE TRICK IS FINDING A WAY TO INTERACT WITH OUTSIDE BOARD MEMBERS WITHOUT OBVIOUSLY CAMPAIGNING FOR A PROMOTION AND WITHOUT THREATENING YOUR BOSS.

Let me tell you about a moment when I was grateful for my own discretion—the moment I learned that my boss and I had shared the same hair-cutter for years. I'd never even suspected it, although that's understandable, given how much less hair this boss had than me.

Now hair stylists are the great amateur psychologists of the service world. I'd bet they hear more secrets even than bartenders. Fortunately, I had never said anything derogatory about my boss, but one day the hair stylist told me he'd heard that I was a difficult person.

"How is that?" I asked.

He wouldn't name names, but he indicated that he also cut the hair of one of my employees.

It wasn't hard to figure out who. I started the next staff meeting by looking around to see who'd recently had a trim. Ted, one of my finance guys, was looking particularly neat that day.

The hair stylist, of course, loved the entire scenario: My boss goes there, I go there, and Ted goes there too.

I was by far the quietest of the group, but now I was afraid to leave the hair stylist anyway. If I did, information would then go directly from Ted to my boss with no filter, other than a hair stylist resentful to have lost me as a client.

 RANDOM STRANGERS TO YOU ARE NOT ALWAYS STRANGERS TO THE PEOPLE WHO HOLD YOUR CAREER IN THEIR HANDS.

I was trapped. I accepted it because it's amazing how stuff carries from ear to ear, truly amazing. And with influential outsiders, you have to try to control your own fate as much as you possibly can.

POSITION

Get into Place, Whether You Are a Hunter,
Skinner, or Diner

Go away fwom here and stop making
all dat noise or I'ww have you
twansferred to the stix!

Tweety Bird

When I first started working at John Hancock, I had enormous respect for the CEO at the time, a man named Jack McElwee. He had been a fighter pilot in World War II, so he arrived at the bubble world of executive success with an unusual amount of life experience. Jack told me once that upward motion in a career usually occurs when an organization is shaking for some reason or another. "There's often a domino effect," he said. "So never be out of position."

I was only 34 when he gave me that piece of advice, and I didn't quite know what it meant.

But I began to learn over the years. First, I learned that you never know what is going to happen in an organization. I've already mentioned that one of my colleagues was killed in a hunting accident. He was only one man, but change rippled through the organization as soon as he was gone. He'd been on track to possibly be the next president. Suddenly, somebody else was running his division, somebody else was heir apparent to the presidency, and other people were moving in to replace the replacements. As Jack had said, there was indeed a domino effect.

Second, I learned that when the dominoes start shifting, luck favors those people who have already begun maneuvering themselves into the positions they want. Because I'd already declared myself as wanting a big revenue job, I was not out of position when that shotgun went off. So I was given more revenue responsibilities, which put me on track to rise.

In other words, I was able to move from "diner" to "hunter," a step up in the modern organizational caste system, which hasn't progressed very far from the caste system in your average Neanderthal cave.

Let me explain: There are three kinds of people in any organization. First, there are the hunters, who go out with

LUCK FAVORS THOSE PEOPLE WHO HAVE ALREADY BEGUN MANEUVERING THEMSELVES INTO THE POSITIONS THEY WANT.

their spears and then bring home the meat that feeds the entire tribe. These are the great fund-raisers and salespeople, the ones who know how to drive money into the organization's coffers.

THE MODERN ORGANIZATIONAL CASTE SYSTEM HASN'T PROGRESSED VERY FAR FROM THE CASTE SYSTEM IN YOUR AVERAGE NEANDERTHAL CAVE.

The skinners, on the other hand, are the ones who take the meat, weigh it, dole it out, store it, and trade it—in other words, the financial types. The smartest of them will figure out how to increase the tribe's wealth, too, by cleverly managing expenses and making deals.

Then there are the diners, the ones who get to eat the hunters' meat because they perform some other useful function for the tribe, such as public relations, or lawyering, or human resources.

Of the three groups, the hunters are always given the greatest respect and the widest possible berth. After all, they are the ones with the sharp, pointed spears. They are always first in line for the top jobs, and they are listened to even when what they have to say is not worth hearing. In fact, the tolerance for hunters in most organizations is absolutely remarkable to me, exceeding even our tolerance as a culture for celebrities like Paris Hilton, Britney Spears, and Lindsay Lohan.

Like starlets, hunters don't have to be smart or politically astute or genuine or sober or graceful as long as they generate a lot of cash.

For example, I remember being in Paris at the Ritz Hotel with a senior salesperson in my organization. Not a particularly sophisticated guy, and you could not be in a more sophisticated hotel. We were having cocktails in the lobby before dinner when he looked around thoughtfully. "Sitting here reminds me of being in Europe," he said.

Paris, of course, would be in Europe. And the evening went downhill from there.

Now, how people as witless as this can close a $100 million sale or squeeze $25 million in donations out of old money is a mystery known only to whatever god you believe in. But in every arena, these people are the rock stars.

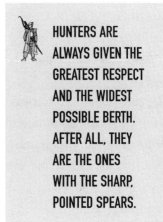

HUNTERS ARE ALWAYS GIVEN THE GREATEST RESPECT AND THE WIDEST POSSIBLE BERTH. AFTER ALL, THEY ARE THE ONES WITH THE SHARP, POINTED SPEARS.

The intellectuals may sit around and say, "Well, that guy's got 40 IQ points less than I do. Here I am teaching nuclear physics, but he's making $7 million a year. There's something wrong." The answer is, there's nothing wrong. Society rewards what society rewards.

So what do you do if you've never bagged a bear or two? What if you're a skinner or a diner?

STOP WHINING! GO HUNT!

It's not impossible to rise to the top of an organization as a diner or a skinner. Just unlikely.

If, for example, you are a very, very good financial analyst, that is how you will be typecast. You may rise within your organization's financial function, but nobody will instantly think of you as the person who should be running a large business.

That said, this is an era of highly complex financing and accounting—and accounting scandals—so good skinners have come to command somewhat more respect in recent years. They, too, can deliver gold. They're just more like alchemists than hunters. They figure out some tax loophole or investment method to turn lead into gold. These days, you will occasionally see a CFO promoted into the CEO's job without a lot of operating experience.

But the diners? People who are diners have a much harder time because they're the spenders in organizational life. They're spending money on advertising, on computer equipment, on real estate, or on legal advice. While they tend to be very smart, it's easy for people to ignore their contributions—even to be a bit suspicious of the money that flows out through them.

And people are naturally inclined to pick the person who feeds them as their leader, rather than the person who designs a new lure or finds a new cave.

Of course, diners can rise on their own track to the highest level in their area of expertise, becoming the general counsel, chief marketing officer, or chief information officer. If they have any talent, they can be in those jobs a very long time, and some people are satisfied with that. But when it comes to running a large business, even the highest-ranked diners are out of position.

Generally, they have no chance of making it to the top of the organization, except if the organization has a severe lack of hunters or a scandal that temporarily makes other things, like reputation, seem more important than meat. This clearly happened at Citigroup in 2002 when the company was reeling from a series of scandals and attracting the unwanted attention of New York State Attorney General Eliot Spitzer. Citigroup CEO Sandy Weill decided it was time for a new head of the corporate and investment bank and turned to Citigroup's top lawyer, Charles Prince.

 IT'S NOT IMPOSSIBLE TO RISE TO THE TOP OF AN ORGANIZATION AS A DINER OR A SKINNER. JUST UNLIKELY.

In his autobiography, Weill says that Prince was "an unproven commodity, having never run a line unit on his own." But Weill wanted to take a chance on him anyway: "If anyone could reason with the regulators, it was Chuck, thanks to his long-standing ties with most of the principal players and his ability to articulate our reforms."

Prince did a good job of defusing the scandals and was named CEO of the whole of Citigroup the next year. Unfortunately, he retired under pressure in late 2007 amid massive losses in the subprime mortgage mess. But for a few years at least, he was the king.

If you are a diner, I wouldn't count on being anointed in a similar fashion. Being a really talented diner is like being a remote prince in the Netherlands who's fifteenth in line for the English throne. Yes, you could become king, but first, the 14 people in front of you would have to go. Now, it's possible that the plague will wipe out everybody in London and you'll become king, but you'll

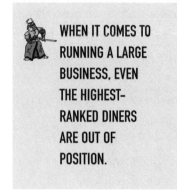

WHEN IT COMES TO RUNNING A LARGE BUSINESS, EVEN THE HIGHEST-RANKED DINERS ARE OUT OF POSITION.

only become king by default. So it makes no sense to sit in the Netherlands telling yourself, "You know what, I'm going to be the king of England because of the fantastic things I've done here in the Netherlands."

My advice to diners and skinners is, go hunt something. If a revenue-gathering job is not on your résumé when the next big job opens up, you have deselected yourself.

However, don't expect people to come around and hold out a Halloween basket for you so that you can pick whatever revenue-generating job you want. Put yourself into position. Make it known that you want a revenue-gathering job. Don't just raise your hand when a job comes up, when people are already thinking of other candidates. Raise your hand in advance.

Then dive right in. If it turns out that you have no appetite for the hunt, you can always come back to the staff job later.

IF A REVENUE-GATHERING JOB IS NOT ON YOUR RÉSUMÉ WHEN THE NEXT BIG JOB OPENS UP, YOU HAVE DESELECTED YOURSELF.

I remember a couple of guys from the dining side at John Hancock, lawyers, smart guys, who wound up running a large and highly sophisticated customer-service operation for us.

They certainly didn't wait for the day that we'd say, "We have two openings here. Are you possibly interested?" Certainly, nobody in top management walked down to the fifty-fifth floor of the Hancock Tower and said, "Hey, let's grab a couple of lawyers to run this business."

But they were given a chance to hunt because they'd asked for it earlier. It was a risk for us, but we decided in the end that they had the management skill set required, so it just might work.

 IF YOU WANT TO BEAT THE HUNTERS AMONG YOUR PEERS, DON'T SIMPLY DRAG HOME THE CARCASS. MANAGE THE ENTIRE HUNT WITH THE SOPHISTICATION OF AN AMERICAN INDIAN.

Well, they went off and did a very good job, energized the division's employees, and saved us a lot of money. Because they'd taken something totally outside the role in which they'd been typecast, in the future they were considered for many other different kinds of jobs and did very well in the company.

Like these lawyers, I'd started at John Hancock as a diner, as a communications person. I could have risen by taking on more staff responsibilities. But I knew how to hunt from my previous life in the advertising and public relations agency business—and I also knew how much hunting was valued when it came time to pass out promotions. So I made it very clear that I wanted revenue-generating responsibilities.

After 1987, I never took another staff job unless it had a substantial revenue-generating portion. I also never gave up the revenue portions of my job when I was promoted. I refused. I wouldn't hand those opportunities off to a competitor. And because I was in revenue-generating roles the few times that the dominoes shifted at John Hancock, I was given the big jobs that put me on track to someday run the organization.

IT'S NOT JUST ABOUT THE MEAT—IT'S ABOUT THE GRAVY AND THE FUR COAT

It's very hard to argue with someone who keeps dropping elk carcasses in the cave. He is sustaining everyone else. But just because that person has earned some respect does not mean that he is a leader.

If you want to beat the hunters among your peers, don't simply drag home the carcass. Manage the entire hunt with the sophistication of an American Indian. Make your own bows, and have your own people trail the herd and determine which animals to kill for the most meat at the least expense to the tribe. Figure out how to make warm clothes out of the hides after the meal is over. Maximize the use of what you've hunted.

The essential weakness of many hunters is that they see everything as a sales job. Yet they may actually have a P&L job, where they are expected not just to bring in revenue but also to generate a profit from it. The problem is that they don't think of it as a P&L job. They say to themselves, "If I find a way to bring money into the company, someone else should figure out a way to make a profit from it." They rely on the organization's skinners to do all the brainwork: "You guys price the product and tell me how much of it I have to sell, and then I'll sell a ton of it."

THE RAP ON HUNTERS IS THAT THEY'LL TRY TO SELL ANYTHING. THEY HAVE NO VISION. THEY'RE RECKLESS.

Now, to really run a P&L business well, you need all kinds of other skills besides the ability to sell. You need to be able to develop products, price them properly, and market them. You have to become a general management person—and that is precisely the kind of person who is most in demand when the board and the CEO go looking for someone for a big job.

In other words, they are looking for judgment as well as strength. The rap on hunters is that they'll try to sell anything, they have no vision, they're reckless. So to rise to the top, you will have to demonstrate some restraint and stay out of the wrong businesses.

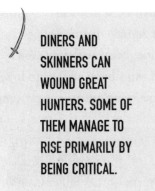

DINERS AND SKINNERS CAN WOUND GREAT HUNTERS. SOME OF THEM MANAGE TO RISE PRIMARILY BY BEING CRITICAL.

I was in an organization once where we had this fantastic person driving sales. Let's call him Andy. It was almost a foregone conclusion that Andy was going to be CEO. But he did not become CEO because of a woman named Rita, who learned how to make money for the company through her own skills as a skinner. She dropped expenses dramatically, developed relationships with clients that made those clients more profitable for us, and showed good judgment for the kinds of ventures we should pursue.

Slowly, she demonstrated the breath of wisdom that overcame the most formidable hunter.

BEWARE THE PASSIVE-AGGRESSIVES

Even those diners and skinners who are not nearly as effective as Rita can wound great hunters. Some of them manage to rise primarily by being critical. They show that the hunters are making so many mistakes, the only safe thing to do is to appoint people who won't make mistakes— namely, them.

If you're a hunter, you can be undermined by an ambitious lawyer who questions your ethics or by an ambitious human resources person who questions your leadership skills. But the skinners are particularly dangerous in that they have all the numbers at their disposal.

I've seen it happen a number of times: A hunter spends a year and a half putting together a product. He has priced it, and he has run models against it. The sales force is eagerly anticipating it.

Yet, right before its final approval, a top level skinner emerges out of the shadows and starts to cast doubt on it. "Our models show that the profit lines aren't quite what you're suggesting," the skinner may say. She then sketches scenarios that suggest that the hunter is not looking at all the possibilities. Or that he is being irresponsible. And it's a way of running him down.

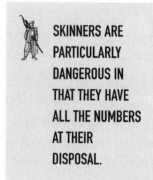

SKINNERS ARE PARTICULARLY DANGEROUS IN THAT THEY HAVE ALL THE NUMBERS AT THEIR DISPOSAL.

There is only one way to fight back: You need to have the right allies. Among your financial people, you must have somebody who can hit the ball with the same velocity as the CFO of the company. Who can come back instantly—certainly within a day—to prove why the CFO's models are wrong. Your lawyer has to be as good the general counsel. Somebody on your staff had better be as sharp as the head of human resources.

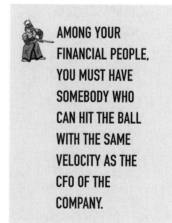

AMONG YOUR FINANCIAL PEOPLE, YOU MUST HAVE SOMEBODY WHO CAN HIT THE BALL WITH THE SAME VELOCITY AS THE CFO OF THE COMPANY.

What you cannot afford to do, even as a great hunter, is underestimate the passive-aggressive powers of the skinners and diners. They can stop you in your tracks, particularly now that there is a post-Enron flight to safety on the part of boards. Directors don't want to offer power to anybody who might embarrass the company or, heaven forfend, bring down the regulators.

There are lots of kings and queens getting knocked off chessboards these days. So beware of pawns who may turn out to be dominating players.

HAVE AN EXIT STRATEGY

It's crucial not just to get into position within your organization, but also in the world at large. That's because a career track that seems perfectly clear today can change overnight. Some limited shock, such as a new boss who fails to see your abilities, may block your way forward.

Then there are the true earthquakes, such as a scandal, a merger, or the collapse of a particular line of business, which can turn your organization upside down—and shake you loose from the chandelier. We are living in a time of tectonic unease, and these catastrophes are not as rare as people comfortable in their careers would like to pretend.

> I'VE SEEN MANY, MANY PEOPLE IN DETERIORATING ORGANIZATIONS THAT WERE ABOUT TO BE SOLD, BUSTED UP, GO BANKRUPT, OR GET MERGED SIT THERE AS IF THEY WERE WATCHING A MOVIE INSTEAD OF BEING ONE OF THE PRINCIPAL ACTORS.

There are usually warning rumbles, and you need to pay attention to them. As I mentioned earlier, in the early 1980s, I was with Commercial Credit, a commercial and consumer lender and insurer. Rather than investing in the business, our parent company, Control Data, was taking capital out whenever it needed it in Minneapolis, which was lowering our bond ratings. Well, excuse me, the handwriting was on the wall there. It was clear to me that if the parent corporation couldn't turn itself around, it was eventually going to sell us. So I began looking for another job.

Yet I've seen many, many people in deteriorating organizations that were about to be sold, busted up, go bankrupt, or get merged sit there as if they were watching a movie instead of being one of the principal actors. They are paralyzed. Even really smart people often don't see upheaval coming, and a lot of them don't wake up even after they lose their job.

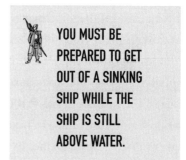

YOU MUST BE PREPARED TO GET OUT OF A SINKING SHIP WHILE THE SHIP IS STILL ABOVE WATER.

It's completely remarkable to me that adults will actually lie around feeling sorry for themselves because there was a merger and the new bosses booted them out with a year's salary. Sometimes they are completely devastated, as if they'd lost their entire family, and are never the same again.

That is ridiculous. You must be prepared to get out of a sinking ship while the ship is still above water, because if hundreds of you are suddenly thrown off at the same time, you're just another head among many bobbing in the sea.

I suggest that you start positioning yourself in the wider world today.

BUILD A NETWORK ON THE OUTSIDE

Get to know people outside your organization. From very early in my career, I've served on nonprofit boards, including the boards of universities, arts organizations, and hospitals.

I never bothered serving on the boards of other corporations, assuming that I would just meet the usual suspects there. But on nonprofit boards, I met people from different walks of life—environmental lawyers, scholars, scientists, philanthropists, theater impresarios—and there is no question that they broadened my horizons.

I also learned to build a reputation for leadership by doing good for my community. When I say "doing good," I don't just mean something passive, like writing the right checks. I mean making things happen in John Hancock's hometown of Boston and being unafraid to express an opinion about what is best for the place.

For example, when elite runners were beginning to bypass the Boston Marathon in the mid-1980s because the race offered no prizes, I persuaded the race organizer, the Boston Athletic Association, to accept its first real sponsor in John Hancock and assured them that we'd enhance the prestige of the race, not exploit it crassly. The sponsorship really did a lot for me within John Hancock by adding a new luster to our brand. But it did even more on the outside. By helping to save a great civic institution, I became somebody to be reckoned with in the city.

 THESE PEOPLE YOU MEET OUTSIDE YOUR ORGANIZATION CAN PROVE VERY VALUABLE IF YOU FIND YOURSELF SHAKEN LOOSE IN SOME ORGANIZATIONAL UPHEAVAL.

In March of 2002, I was also the first business leader in Boston to call for the resignation of Cardinal Bernard Law, as the extent of his failure to protect children from known pedophiles in the priesthood was becoming clear. I wrote an op-ed piece for the *Boston Globe* using the Cardinal's own words against him and saying it was time for a new "pastor and teacher and father." It made me unpopular with some people, but others were grateful that I'd spoken out.

The fact that I was never afraid to say what I thought in defense of the community made politicians, I think, much more comfortable with me than they are with many business executives. As a result, I had a wide and diverse network of outsiders to call on.

Expand your network also by spreading your business around, as I mentioned in the section on vendors. Don't just get to know the people at one law firm. Get to know the people at three or five.

These people you meet outside your organization can prove very valuable if you find yourself shaken loose in some organizational upheaval. They can also help you build a favor bank the size of Lake Erie. You will always know the right person to call, no matter what kind of help somebody needs.

Become well known as a person who can get something done. Almost never ask for a favor in return, and I promise you, you will be repaid amply when you really need it. A lot of executives make the mistake of thinking the favor system works only one way—in *their* favor—and they don't understand why, at some point, the goodwill dries up.

> BECOME WELL KNOWN AS A PERSON WHO CAN GET SOMETHING DONE. ALMOST NEVER ASK FOR A FAVOR IN RETURN, AND YOU WILL BE REPAID AMPLY WHEN YOU REALLY NEED IT.

That's just foolish. I've collected so many chits over the years, I find that, even in retirement, there is almost no one who won't take my phone call.

STAY FREE

Even with a rich favor bank behind you, you may find that when you're pulled off one organizational breast, there isn't necessarily another one to latch onto instantly. When you get into the mid- to high-six-figure kinds of jobs, there simply are not that many of them out there.

> MAKE SURE THAT YOU ARE AS FINANCIALLY INDEPENDENT AS YOU CAN POSSIBLY BE.

I suggest, first, making sure that you are as financially independent as you can possibly be. If you cannot take care of your financial obligations—at least temporarily—without a steady paycheck from some organization, you may end up taking a job you don't want and then staying in that job because you don't want the tenure to seem too short on your résumé. You may well wind up sacrificing three years of your career only to find that you're off track when you are ready to move on. Don't cultivate habits that will make you dependent.

> BUILD A REPUTATION AS AN EXPERT IN SOME AREA. WRITE ARTICLES. GIVE SPEECHES. LET REPORTERS QUOTE YOU.

Second, work out a plan in case you lose your job. I always had a plan for what I would do if I got fired, and it never involved sand or water or sun.

Make sure, as you develop your skills as a general manager, that you also develop some particular marketable skill. For example, I could start a brand management consultancy tomorrow. Build a reputation as an expert in some area. Write articles. Give speeches. Let reporters quote you.

Then, if you do lose your berth, you will be able to convince at least a handful of other organizations to pay you for advice and counsel.

If you're good, and I'm assuming you are, at least one of those organizations will eventually decide that they are paying you too much as a consultant and offer you a big job with them. It happens all the time, and that is a very pleasant position to find yourself in.

CULTURE

Before You Sign on, Make Sure It's a Culture, Not a Cult

It's not wise to violate rules until you know how to observe them.

T. S. Eliot

C*ulture* is one of the more overused words in American business. It's true that all organizations, like it or not, have a culture. It's also true that the actual culture of a place only rarely corresponds to the things the CEO and top management say about it.

For example, in the founders' letter attached to its IPO prospectus, Google made one of the bolder cultural statements in recent history: "Don't be evil." Then, in 2006, Google did something less than saintly: It agreed to censor its Internet search results in the People's Republic of China in order to please the Chinese government.

At least Google founders Larry Page and Sergey Brin have the wit to laugh a little at their own sloganeering. When asked at the 2007 Global Philanthropy Forum conference about "Don't be evil," Brin joked, "A lot of people misinterpret that. They miss the implicit second-person subject, because, of course, we're not evil. It's *you* don't be evil. We're speaking to the rest of the world. So, to enforce this concept . . . Larry, tell them about the laser."

"Culture" is a convenient little weapon for many organizational leaders. Some invoke it when they want to set arbitrary rules for their people: "We don't turn off our cell phones, ever. We're a 24/7 culture."

Other bosses use the concept to pat themselves on the back. "It's not our culture here to openly show your ambitions," they might say. "We're all team players." Meanwhile, the place is full of piranhas.

People constantly make stuff up and call it a culture. And the mission statements that somehow embody the goals of this culture? They take months, if not years, to write, and a committee to do it, and usually there is tremendous back and forth, and lots of emphasis on bringing the highest-quality services to clients worldwide while also being the highest-quality workplace. Meanwhile, nobody mentions the underlying ruthlessness that characterizes most organizations.

PEOPLE CONSTANTLY MAKE STUFF UP AND CALL IT A CULTURE.

I recently called somebody on this. I was having a bite to eat while I was traveling and wound up sitting next to somebody who worked for a mutual fund company. We talked a bit about how little the financial services industry reflects the diversity of America. "Companies have ways of not hiring minorities," I said, "by simply saying they can't find qualified minorities."

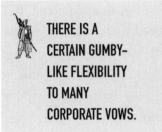

THERE IS A CERTAIN GUMBY-LIKE FLEXIBILITY TO MANY CORPORATE VOWS.

He then told me a story about trying to recruit a candidate from North Carolina, a person of color. They'd spent so much time on it that when the guy ultimately decided not to come to work for them, they'd given up on the idea.

It was a very weak-livered excuse. "Did you ever ask the person," I asked, "what it was going to take to get him to join your company? Offer him another $30,000?"

"No," the guy said. "I can't make my numbers if I give away money."

"Well, I assume your mission statement says how committed you are to a diverse workplace."

"Sure, but how could I justify to my shareholders paying this person $30,000 more than I would pay someone else in the same position?"

"Your shareholders have bought into your mission statement, too, so you shouldn't have to justify it to them. But what you are really saying to me is that you don't really practice what you preach."

He shrugged.

There is a certain Gumby-like flexibility to many corporate vows.

This is not to say that all cultural claims are nonsense. Some organizations really do build powerful cultures that serve them well for a long time. IBM in its mainframe-era heyday was a terrific example. In his book *Who Says Elephants Can't Dance? Inside IBM's Historic Turnaround*, former CEO Lou Gerstner points out that IBM's stated ideal of respect for its employees actually made IBM uniquely progressive: "IBM was the leader in diversity for decades, well before governments even spoke of the need to seek equality in employment, advancement, and compensation."

Shaped by its two most influential leaders, Thomas Watson, Sr., and Thomas Watson, Jr., IBM's culture was one of almost militaristic regimentation coupled with a paternalistic concern for its people, who were lifers. Everyone at IBM dressed alike in the corporate equivalent of the Mao suit—white shirt, rep tie, wingtips, and dark blue suit. The organization spent a lot of time and effort developing the skills of its managers and inculcating its values. It was a culture of excellence that said, if you want to work with us, you have to join up. If you want to buy from us, you have to join up.

If you want to buy from someone else? You are on your own.

This culture created an aura that only reinforced IBM's dominance in the computer business. Since IBM was so clearly the gold standard, every IT officer in the world felt safe buying IBM. They all knew that if something went wrong, those impeccable IBMers would work their tails off to fix it.

Whether the "culture" of your organization is a real way of behaving and thinking that brings out the best in people or nothing more than organized hypocrisy, you must pay attention to a few things when you move into senior management.

WHETHER THE "CULTURE" OF YOUR ORGANIZATION IS A REAL WAY OF BEHAVING AND THINKING THAT BRINGS OUT THE BEST IN PEOPLE OR NOTHING MORE THAN ORGANIZED HYPOCRISY, YOU MUST PAY ATTENTION TO IT WHEN YOU MOVE INTO MANAGEMENT.

First, you must know the unwritten rules of your organization's culture so that you don't break them unwittingly.

Second, you must consider whether or not the culture is one that will reward your efforts.

Third, you have to make sure that the culture doesn't wind up warping you in ways that will damage your career.

Fourth, to be a leader, you have to try to influence the culture in positive ways.

EVEN IN THE TWENTY-FIRST CENTURY, THERE ARE STILL TABOOS

The first thing you have to understand about your organization's culture is its taboos. Otherwise, you can be smacked in the head for something you naively think is good—or rejected completely, like a donor organ the body may desperately need but does not want. Until you are CEO—and are CEO for a good long time—if there is a serious conflict between you and the culture, the culture usually wins.

Consider the sorry case of Julie Roehm at Wal-Mart, who was brought in as a senior vice president for marketing communications in 2006 to enliven Wal-Mart's image. She'd made a name for herself at Chrysler by conceiving racy commercials and sponsorships. Unfortunately, working at a desperate-for-attention American car company is not the same as working at the dominant, conservative, proud company of Sam Walton.

First, Wal-Mart pulled a commercial Roehm had developed showing a husband giving his wife lingerie for Christmas, after just a couple of complaints. *New York Magazine* reported that the company wasn't happy, either, when the new advertising agency she'd chosen after a long review published an ad in a trade magazine featuring lions copulating, with the tag line, "It's good to be on top."

Within a year, Roehm was fired, and bitter recriminations soon followed on both sides, with Wal-Mart accusing her of everything from having an inappropriate relationship with a subordinate, to violating its gratuities policy by accepting a case of vodka from the agency, to sitting on the lap of an agency executive at Nobu 57, a high-end sushi restaurant in New York.

Vodka, sushi, inappropriate relationship—it was entirely too lively for Bentonville, Arkansas. Roehm told *BusinessWeek* what she'd learned: "The importance of culture. It can't be underestimated."

If you are new to an organization, you can be as conservative as a nun and still unwittingly break some taboos. For example, how do you decide where to hold an off-site meeting for your group? If you choose the Holiday Inn on one of the beltways surrounding your city and your peers all choose Hawaii, you may appear to the powers-that-be to be suspiciously low-rent, and it can hurt you. On the other hand, if you bring your senior staff and their spouses to Hawaii, in some organizations that would be considered an outrageous waste of money. And you'd be punished for it.

> IF YOU ARE NEW TO AN ORGANIZATION, YOU CAN BE AS CONSERVATIVE AS A NUN AND STILL UNWITTINGLY BREAK SOME TABOOS.

You have to be aware of the cultural taboos in the way you treat your employees, too. How much process do you have to have before you fire somebody? How much latitude do you have in rewarding somebody else?

What is the behavior in meetings? In some companies, you're allowed to take out a long knife with your bosses present, and in other cultures, if you take out a long knife, you may as well commit hara-kiri.

When you rise to the senior level, there is even more of an expectation that you will demonstrate whatever the culture is and that it will cascade down from you. At the same time, you may find that the culture is different at the top, with its own set of taboos. The rules change.

For example, in certain cultures, the middle managers make all the presentations. The senior executives talk less but listen more and then make their decisions. If you become a senior executive in a culture like this but insist on talking a lot, you'll be seen as somebody who still belongs in middle management.

When I first moved up to the top floor at John Hancock, I didn't realize that you didn't just pop in on people, although there were only seven or eight offices there. You called each other or wrote to make appointments. In middle management, on the other hand, a guy's down the hall, the door's open, you knock on the door and say, "Are you busy, Charlie?"

> **WHEN YOU RISE TO THE SENIOR LEVEL, THERE IS EVEN MORE OF AN EXPECTATION THAT YOU WILL DEMONSTRATE WHATEVER THE CULTURE IS AND THAT IT WILL CASCADE DOWN FROM YOU.**

There was a certain formality in John Hancock's culture at the top, only I didn't entirely grasp it. Somebody finally told me, "Don't just drop down here. That's not how we do things on this floor." And it was okay. I got it—before I'd embarrassed myself for too long.

I'm not saying never violate an organizational taboo. Some of them need violating. Just make sure you do it deliberately and with forethought.

WHAT ARE THE CHANCES OF THE CULTURE VALUING YOUR CONTRIBUTIONS?

There are a lot of very bad organizational cultures out there. While they go bad for many reasons, the underlying cause is always the cultural myopia that develops when the people on the inside become so focused on themselves that they forget that the outside world judges things differently.

Even the great culture of IBM, which worked brilliantly when IBM had a near-monopoly on the computer business, became so arrogant and self-absorbed by the early 1990s that, in a much more democratic computer marketplace, it nearly brought the company to its knees.

Lou Gerstner, who took over in 1993, describes the problem vividly in *Who Says Elephants Can't Dance?*:

> To someone arriving at IBM from the outside, there was a kind of hothouse quality to the place. It was like an isolated tropical ecosystem that had been cut off from the world too long. . . . This hermetically sealed quality—an institutional viewpoint that anything important started inside the company—was, I believe, the root cause of many of our problems.

Gerstner wound up shocking a lot of IBMers by reminding them that business is a competitive endeavor and that outside the hothouse, the competition was beating them viciously.

The problem with working in a self-absorbed culture is that its leaders stop responding to normal stimuli like competition and opportunity—and talent and ambition—and fixate only on their own obsessions. So if you offer what would normally be seen as a fantastic array of abilities, in the wrong culture, they may be ignored or even punished.

Cultures tend to devolve especially quickly in places where the top people all think alike. For example, I once worked at a place where the cronyism among the leadership was just remarkable. They'd all known each other for years, they'd all had similar upbringings and training, and they were all utopians who believed answering society's unmet needs was their primary mission. That once very successful company has now vanished into the sands of history, thanks to the foolish decisions of this tight-knit group.

THE PROBLEM WITH WORKING IN A SELF-ABSORBED CULTURE IS THAT ITS LEADERS STOP RESPONDING TO NORMAL STIMULI AND FIXATE ONLY ON THEIR OWN OBSESSIONS.

I'll never forget the first time I had to go up to the executive floor there. I was waiting in my best suit and shirt when a couple of the company's most senior people walked in, in hunting gear, with shotguns and dead fowl over their shoulders. There was a forest near headquarters, and the top executives would hunt there together.

The guy I was going to meet with threw his dead birds on his secretary's desk and said, "Have the kitchen clean these."

I found this very odd indeed. What kind of people go hunting on a weekday and then walk through the lobby carrying shotguns? Worse, what kind of people send out memos about being an equal opportunity employer for women and then throw bloody ducks on a secretary's desk? Yet these were the people telling me what to do.

Another time, the company suddenly anointed a long-time employee without a strong background in marketing as worldwide head of marketing and sales. I'd never met the guy. Let's call him Fritz and speculate that he got the job because he was an old jousting pal of the king's—and possibly smart enough to fall off the horse at the first tip of the king's lance.

Since this firm had been buying so many companies and combining them, the leadership decided to take over a golf resort for two weeks, have a series of sales and marketing conventions there one after another, and just roll people through them. And Fritz would display himself in his new role there.

At the first of these conventions, there was, as usual, a grand parade of dull speeches made by people justifying their existence, with the poor slide makers working long into the night making slides for them, and the audience suffering through every excruciating minute.

It was 95 degrees outside, but we were all buttoned up in suits and ties and perpetually nursing the hangovers from hell because the company always scheduled a big dinner event and kept us up drinking long into the night. Then the first presentation of the day was always at 7 a.m., to ensure that the meeting had enough business content to be tax-deductible—but still allow the whole afternoon for golf.

On just such a miserable morning, the new mucky-muck was finally introduced. And out onto the stage steps Fritz—a pudgy 50-year-old guy in Tyrolean lederhosen and a funny little hat with a feather on it.

We laughed. We literally thought it was a joke. Sometimes they do these little jokes to wake you up. The guy looked like Benny Hill. How could this possibly be the guy? But no, Fritz offered some lame explanation for his attire—he was very proud of his European heritage—and then launched into a serious speech.

No one heard a word that he said, they were so fixated on his hat and his knees. And he continued to make the same entrance four or five times as different groups moved through. What did Fritz's European heritage have to do with the challenges of our business? Nothing, but that's what he was focused on.

Through that single act of symbolism, he probably made hundreds of people question what kind of company they were with. And this eccentric continued to have enormous influence over the company for a very long time as it concentrated on everything but its core business and frittered away its market share.

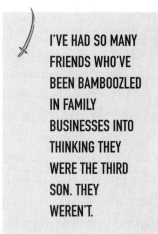

I'VE HAD SO MANY FRIENDS WHO'VE BEEN BAMBOOZLED IN FAMILY BUSINESSES INTO THINKING THEY WERE THE THIRD SON. THEY WEREN'T.

There used to be a group within John Hancock that was just as odd. They were notoriously cheap, personally cheap, and cheap with the company's money, too. They were the kind of people who wore monogrammed shirts, only with someone else's monogram, because they'd bought them second-hand. One time I went to a meeting with the people in this group. The meeting was scheduled to end at noon, so a lunch wasn't planned. But it was getting to be around 1 p.m., and we'd been working since 8 a.m. without a crumb.

KEEP YOUR EYES OPEN TO THE CULTURE IN WHICH YOU ARE WORKING, AND MAKE SURE THAT IT WON'T REJECT YOU UNJUSTLY.

So the most senior person in the room reached into his pocket and pulled out a tunafish sandwich.

He looked innocently around at the rest of us. "You guys didn't bring your lunch?" he asked.

It made me think he had actually planned the meeting to go longer than he'd said and just didn't want to pay for lunch for everybody. That bothered me. But what really bothered me was the fact that the sandwich had been in his pocket—unwrapped!

These people were loathe to spend money even to make money. Now, when it came to their own compensation, this group was remarkably tenacious. Their defense was, we're such a cost-conscious crowd that even in those years when we are not making a lot of money for the company, we deserve to get bonuses.

To me, the fact that they were unwilling to spend company money on anything, even the smartest investment, did not mean they were wise. It meant they were cheap. If you are a risk taker, run the other way rather than take a job in a culture like this.

Family-owned businesses are particularly prone to cultural myopia because all the power is generally in one person's hands. The culture is whatever the *pater familias* says it is. He doesn't have to worry about boards of directors and shareholders. He doesn't have to think about how he is going to be viewed by outsiders. So he can be despotic.

I've had so many friends who've been bamboozled in family businesses into thinking they were the third son. They weren't. The fact is, unless you are the son or daughter, you are nothing more than hired help, and you will probably never get to fulfill your ambitions in that company.

Consider the privately held Fidelity Investments. Even though Chairman Ned Johnson is in his late seventies, the people in the top jobs there tend not to stay for long. *Boston Globe* columnist Steve Bailey put it this way: "Sitting at Ned Johnson's right hand has always been one of the most dangerous jobs in Boston. . . ." Meanwhile, Ned's daughter Abigail is at Fidelity and possibly waiting in the wings. Whether or not she winds up running Fidelity, my point is that this is a very tough place for senior non-Johnsons. One day you are eating caviar there. The next day you are eating curb.

Keep your eyes open to the culture in which you are working, and make sure that it won't reject you unjustly. In certain businesses, clashes between strong executives and the organizations that employ them are a part of life. If you work at a movie studio or are a professional sports coach, it's practically a badge of honor to be fired now and then. In corporate life, though, if you are fired within three years of joining an organization, your career can really be hurt by it.

Be sure also that the culture of your organization allows for forward motion—that it will give you the opportunities you deserve. If not, make a deft exit as soon as you can.

DO NOT BECOME A CULTIST

Far worse than failing to understand the rules in a good culture or failing to be rewarded in a poor culture is being co-opted by a really bad one.

Some cultures devolve into cults because of the force of the CEO or founder's personality. Sometimes a cult of personality makes an organization successful. There's no question that Richard Branson *is* the Virgin Group and Steve Jobs *is* Apple, and their personalities infuse and inspire their businesses. But other times the darker side of a personality rules, and the outcome is less positive.

SOMETIMES A CULT OF PERSONALITY MAKES AN ORGANIZATION SUCCESSFUL.

Enron under Jeff Skilling, the former president and CEO, is a terrific example. Skilling was a Harvard MBA, a McKinsey alum, famously smart and impatient, and Enron clearly remade itself in his image. It became a culture that was arrogant about its own brains, easily bored, restlessly moving from deal to deal, rewarding aggressiveness while never pausing to demand results, unconcerned about expenses, with an overwhelming sense of entitlement.

> A FRAUD AS BIG AS ENRON'S DOES NOT OCCUR WITHOUT HUNDREDS OF PEOPLE KNOWING DEEP DOWN THAT SOMETHING IS WRONG.

Since these were the qualities that were rewarded, it was difficult to work at Enron and not buy into the culture. In their book *The Smartest Guys in the Room: The Amazing Rise and Scandalous Fall of Enron*, authors Bethany McLean and Peter Elkind quote one long-time Enron executive:

> I used to walk off the company plane after being picked up and dropped off by a limousine, and I'd have to remind myself I was a real human being. You start living that life long enough, if you don't have very strong morals, you lose it fast. Enron was the kind of company that could spoil you pretty well.

Enron clearly did spoil a lot of people. A fraud as big as Enron's does not occur without hundreds of people knowing deep down that something is wrong. It's a cultural problem, not just a problem of a few bad apples.

Organizations like Enron are awash in MBAs from Harvard and Stanford. They have auditing teams and risk management departments that know the fundamental rules. They are full of basically honest people. But even smart, honest people can lose perspective when they spend 12 hours a day in these vertical villages, when they have too much faith in the local royalty, and when they grow too much attached to the loot handed out by their leaders.

If you join such a cult, your career can be damaged terribly, even if you yourself do nothing wrong. Even the people who had nothing to do with the accounting fraud at Enron were tainted by the scandal, and many of them had a very hard time finding work after the company collapsed.

Possibly more dangerous than a cult of personality is a culture that has no values at all, except the bottom line. I call this a "loan shark" culture.

When I was a kid, my dad borrowed from loan sharks. The interest was five percent a week, and it had to be paid every week. If the loan shark's collector walked in, and my dad said, "Look, my kid was in the hospital this week. I can't pay you until next week," the collector would say, "I'm really sorry to hear about your kid in the hospital. Pay me my money."

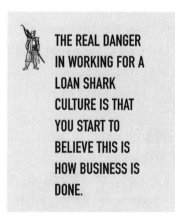

THE REAL DANGER IN WORKING FOR A LOAN SHARK CULTURE IS THAT YOU START TO BELIEVE THIS IS HOW BUSINESS IS DONE.

No matter what anybody said, the refrain was always the same: "Pay me my money."

At some organizations, this attitude is endemic.

If Mrs. Ashford hasn't yet decided whether to donate her $100,000 to your organization and needs a few more weeks of persuading on your part, your bosses may not care. Make the numbers. If the regions you control failed to sell enough because the retailers couldn't get your product on the shelves, your bosses may not care. Make the numbers, make them now, or else.

The real danger in working for a loan shark culture is not the danger of having your legs broken if you don't make your numbers. The real danger is that you start to believe this is how business is done. My advice is, walk away from those kinds of bosses and those kinds of organizations as quickly as possible.

If the consequences of not making your numbers in any quarter, even for good reasons, are awful, you may be tempted to do something unethical to make them. And if you are caught, your career is simply finished.

SHOW THAT YOU ARE NOT DIVORCED FROM REALITY

As you rise, you will begin to influence your own organizational culture. I happen to think it's extraordinarily important not to become a caricature like the one Michael Douglas played in the movie *Wall Street*—the calculator executive who only understands one tongue—the balance sheet.

Of course, the temptation is always there to be numbers-focused and unforgiving, given the intense pressure on returns coming from Wall Street analysts and private equity owners. But you have to remember that the people who work for you—the ones whose efforts help to determine those returns—are generally not there because they want to be. They're there because they have to be.

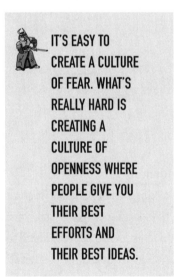

IT'S EASY TO CREATE A CULTURE OF FEAR. WHAT'S REALLY HARD IS CREATING A CULTURE OF OPENNESS WHERE PEOPLE GIVE YOU THEIR BEST EFFORTS AND THEIR BEST IDEAS.

So, if you build a cold, harsh, humorless environment for them, you are doing no more than running a prison, albeit a minimum security prison with tennis court and gym. Your employees will do the very least they can to get by, just enough to avoid solitary and no more.

It's easy to create a culture of fear, in my opinion. What's really hard is creating a culture of openness where people give you their best efforts and their best ideas.

As I rose at John Hancock, there were many good things about the existing culture that I just took advantage of, including the fact that it *was* a culture that allowed for creativity. No one in this culture got punished for having bad ideas. Somebody might say no, but you'd never be punished for proposing something.

I tried to reinforce that freedom. I can remember once in a meeting someone suggested that we target single mothers for life insurance products.

A financial guy jumped on this idea. "Single mothers don't have enough money," he said scornfully.

One senior woman turned to him coolly and asked, "Exactly how many single mothers do you know?"

ORGANIZATIONAL LEADERS, LIKE POLITICIANS, HAVE TO PROVE THEIR HUMANITY.

"Well, there's a single mother who lives down the street from me, and she's really struggling."

The woman said, "So your entire conclusion is based on a survey of one?"

By this point, people were waiting to see what I was going to do. Were we really going to have a fight about what we do and do not know about how people live?

My thought was, let it fly. Let them talk. Let them get agitated. It was a social clash, but with a business purpose. The truth, of course, is that single mothers have an even greater need for life insurance than married couples, and many of them could afford it. So, out of that meeting, we came up with a product for them.

It turned out to be a great thing for our women brokers and agents to sell because single mothers tended to trust women advisors. And we sold a lot of it.

Of course, if you want to create a culture that encourages risk-taking and some healthy dissent, you have to appear reasonably well balanced yourself. If you are wearing lederhosen and a feathered hat whenever you get the chance, that tends not to inspire confidence among the vast majority of your non-lederhosen-wearing employees.

Organizational leaders, like politicians, have to prove their humanity—
or at least that they are not so divorced from reality that they can't recognize good work when they see it.

At John Hancock, the forums we held for all our employees every other
month or so gave me that opportunity. I'd always begin with something
funny. Once I picked someone I didn't
know out of the front row and said, "Do
me a favor. Go to the cafeteria and
count how many people are sitting
there." Everyone was supposed to be at
the forum.

He came back and said, "Fifty five."

I said, "They may be smarter than us.
I'd rather be having a cappuccino, too."
The audience laughed loudly. And no
one *ever* went to the cafeteria again during one of my sessions.

> YOUR EMPLOYEES
> CAN GET A VERY
> GOOD SENSE OF
> WHO YOU ARE IN A
> Q&A. AND WHEN
> YOU DON'T HIDE
> FROM THEM, THEY
> KNOW THEY HAVE A
> LEADER.

The forum would also include a
straightforward presentation of how our businesses were doing. Then I'd
take questions from the audience—silly questions, tricky questions,
embarrassing questions alike.

This was hard to do, as difficult as holding a press conference. But your
employees can get a very good sense of who you are in a Q&A. And when
you don't hide from them, they know they have a leader.

I remember being asked at one forum, "How many hours do you work
a day?"

I answered, "It depends. Some days, 2 hours. Some days, 20. The fact
that I'm in my office 10 hours a day doesn't mean that I'm working all the
time."

This is directly contrary to the myth of the bionic executive who hits
the gym at 4 a.m., is at the office by 5:30 a.m., works all day, heads home
at 6:30 p.m., and then uses the hours after dinner to catch up on the day's

e-mail. Admittedly, there are many different kinds of workaholics, and I was certainly always thinking about the job. But I saw no upside in appearing to be machine-like.

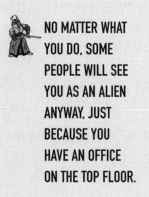

NO MATTER WHAT YOU DO, SOME PEOPLE WILL SEE YOU AS AN ALIEN ANYWAY, JUST BECAUSE YOU HAVE AN OFFICE ON THE TOP FLOOR.

Of course, no matter what you do, some people will see you as an alien anyway, just because you have an office on the top floor. And the rumors can be pretty strange.

One day I was having lunch in the cafeteria. Two women I didn't know were sitting next to me. One of them asked, "Is it true that you have a hot tub in your office?"

I said, "Do you mean a cauldron?" Sadly, the joke was lost on these two.

"Well," she said dismissively, "everybody thinks you have a hot tub in your office."

At John Hancock, we had a simple cultural goal: We wanted to make the company a great place to be *at* and a great place to be *from*.

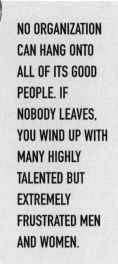

NO ORGANIZATION CAN HANG ONTO ALL OF ITS GOOD PEOPLE. IF NOBODY LEAVES, YOU WIND UP WITH MANY HIGHLY TALENTED BUT EXTREMELY FRUSTRATED MEN AND WOMEN.

A great place to be *at*, in my opinion, is one where there is a free exchange of ideas, where there is some humor and fun, and where people's contributions are rewarded.

Why did we want to make it a great place to be *from*? Because no organization can hang onto all of its good people. There is only one head of marketing slot, only one CFO's job. If nobody leaves, you wind up with many highly talented but extremely frustrated men and women. And no boss says, "Where can I get more of those?"

223

So we wanted our employees to know that if you had John Hancock on your résumé, it would be impressive to future employers. And everything we did to enhance our image, from our community relations to our Olympics sponsorship, was intended to inspire pride in anybody who could say, "I worked at John Hancock."

This wasn't quite as lofty a goal as "Don't be evil" or "Answer society's unmet needs." But I like to think we succeeded—and had a better business for it.

THE NEW BOSSES

It's Not the Same Old Twentieth-Century Game

They couldn't hit an elephant
at this dist…

Union General John Sedgwick's
last words before being killed
by a Confederate sniper

Whether they work in nonprofits or businesses or universities, executives now have to do their jobs in an environment that has changed tremendously in recent years. New media, the wave of scandals that began with Enron, new technologies, and new sources of money with new expectations have produced a Chinese menu of new bosses, each with his or her own agenda.

This is not a complacent group, either. They are aggressive and demanding. You cannot rise to the top of any organization without recognizing these bosses, and you have to manage them intelligently.

Let's take them one by one.

JOURNALISTS—KEEP IT HUMAN IF YOU CAN

As late as 2000, right before the dot-com bubble burst, senior executives in business walked on water. They were heroes in the press. Now they are potential trophies to be hunted, and this is not going to change any time soon.

Soon after the scandals at Enron, WorldCom, and Tyco had unraveled, I guest-hosted the CNBC business show *Squawk Box*. The Wall Street pundits on the show were all saying, "Well, these scandals are over now. Things are getting back to normal."

My response was, "They're not over. They are *never* going to be over."

I believe I was right. The accounting frauds were followed in rapid succession by the Wall Street research scandal; market timing, late trading, and front running in mutual funds; stock-options backdating and other compensation

> SUBTLE PROBLEMS THAT IN THE PAST WOULD HAVE BEEN HANDLED IN A BOARDROOM—IF THEY WERE EVEN FOUND—ARE NOW RESOLVED WITH RAPID FIRINGS AND PUBLIC SHAMINGS IN THE WALL STREET JOURNAL.

scandals; and the subprime mortgage meltdown. Subtle problems that in the past would have been handled in a boardroom—if they were even found—are now resolved with rapid firings, public shamings in the *Wall Street Journal*, investigations, indictments, big fines, and prison.

What has happened to American organizations, thanks to the thuggery of Enron, is the same thing that happened to the American government in the early 1970's, thanks to the thuggery of the Nixon administration. The blind trust of the people is now gone. Watergate ripped the veil off that trust, and so did Enron and friends. People now expect and are entertained by business scandals, as much as they expect and are entertained by political dirty tricks.

At the same time, thanks to cable TV and the Internet, there has been an explosion of news outlets all looking for a good story. If you happen to provide one, you can make a reporter's career. There is also a pack mentality among the press, so if one reporter catches you at something, the entire Fourth Estate follows nipping behind.

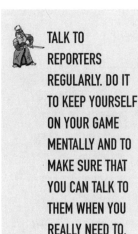

TALK TO REPORTERS REGULARLY. DO IT TO KEEP YOURSELF ON YOUR GAME MENTALLY AND TO MAKE SURE THAT YOU CAN TALK TO THEM WHEN YOU REALLY NEED TO.

As an executive, you now have to be extra careful not to draw the wrong kind of attention to yourself. You can't take a golf trip on a vendor's tab. You have to think twice before offering a contract to a friend. If you are running a museum, you can't buy smuggled antiquities anymore. The rules have changed, and behavior that used to be standard practice is no longer acceptable.

At the same time, senior executives also cannot afford to be ostriches and ignore the press. When you have your head in the sand, that only makes your butt that much more of a target—and you won't see it coming.

I suggest that you talk to reporters regularly. If for no other reason, do it to keep yourself on your game mentally and to make sure that you *can* talk to them when you really need to.

Make no mistake about it. As a senior executive, you may now earn five or ten or twenty times what most reporters make, but I can guarantee you that those reporters were the smartest people in their college classes. They just chose a different path than you did.

These are worthy adversaries. And by middle age, these reporters have seen some of their peers who are not as smart endowing new buildings on college campuses while they are struggling just to pay tuition for their kids. Some of them view this as a great injustice because they consider them-selves truth-tellers and think any righteous society would reward them.

While most of them are scrupulously fair, if they do find a reason to take you down, they may not be entirely sorry.

So be prepared when you talk to them. It's a bad idea to try to squeeze in an inter-view when you are just coming off an air-plane and are tired or in the 15 minutes between meetings. It's an especially bad idea to be unprepared for a television interview, which can then live on in YouTube infamy. Have your staff prepare Q&As for you. Even do a mock interview

> AN INTERVIEW IS A LOT LIKE A GAME OF POOL. IT'S NOT JUST ABOUT MAKING THE SHOT; IT'S ALSO ABOUT SETTING UP THE NEXT SHOT.

with your staff if the interview is very important. Before I appeared on TV, I made sure that I had half an hour alone to think about what I wanted to say.

Don't soliloquize in interviews. Give short answers that cannot be taken out of context. You may even make it a condition of the interview: "Sure, I'll talk to you. But I have one thing I want to say, and you must agree to print it."

Understand, however, that an interview is a lot like a game of pool. It's not just about making the shot; it's also about setting up the next shot. So, while you are answering one question, anticipate the follow-up question because that is the question to be concerned about.

Avoid press conferences unless you have to have one in order to deal with a really bad story or to make an important announcement. Believe it or not, reporters are human, though I'm sure that there have been clinical studies to the contrary. The stories about you will be much more positive if you develop relationships with reporters individually.

It's also important to understand that your press will never be 100 percent positive. The truth is that if you are getting really good press, some reporters will be contrarians just to stand out from the crowd.

Make your own decisions about which reporters to meet with. You cannot depend solely on your public relations people, who are generally working hard to ensure that there is never a single piece of negative publicity about you. But the truth is, even when you know a piece is likely to be negative, you can't keep it from being written just by refusing to give a reporter access. And if you allow the interview, you may influence the coverage for the better. Let's admit, that's human nature. It's much easier to be nasty about someone you haven't met than someone you have.

IF YOU ARE GETTING REALLY GOOD PRESS, SOME REPORTERS WILL BE CONTRARIANS JUST TO STAND OUT FROM THE CROWD.

I can remember one columnist who every few months would write something negative about me. If he couldn't attack the performance of my organization, he'd find a way to attack me personally.

I'd never met him. But finally, I called him up. "This is the jerk you've written badly about," I said.

"Which one?" he laughed.

I told him, then added, "I would like you to buy me a drink."

"Why should I do that?"

"Because you've written terrible things about me. Before you write more terrible things about me, don't you think you should meet me? That way, you can write terrible things about the meeting."

"Okay," he said. "That's worth a drink."

So we met for a beer. "I don't want to talk about your columns," I said.

He was surprised. "You don't?"

"No," I said. "It's America. You can write whatever you want. I just want to show you I'm not quite as bad a guy as you think." So we talked about politics mostly. After that, his coverage was no longer slanted against me. It was straight reporting.

REPORTERS HAVE A RIGHT TO THEIR POINT OF VIEW, AND IT'S NOT ALWAYS SMART TO HOLD IT AGAINST THEM.

It *is* America. Reporters have a right to their point of view, and it's not always smart to hold it against them. If, however, a reporter lies about you or proves that he has an ax to grind, that is a different story. I refuse to talk to somebody like that.

Sometimes, reporters are so determined to tell the story their own slanted way that they'd prefer not to talk to you. There was one reporter who wrote a piece in which he claimed that he'd called me six times for a comment and I'd never responded.

This was a story I *would* have responded to. So I had our phone logs pulled. There were no calls from this reporter—none from his office number, none from his cell number, and none from his home number. I had my PR people call his editor and let the editor know he'd lied in print. He soon left that publication.

Then he went to work at another, where he continued skewering us. We refused to speak to him. Finally, the business editor there called and said, "You can't just ignore us."

Yes, we could. We told him why, and the editor pulled the reporter off our beat.

But such dishonesty is the exception, not the rule. I recommend actually helping reporters out. If they call, on a deadline, looking for some industry perspective, give it to them. You don't have to go on the record. But lend them a hand, including young reporters, because you never know where they will end up. Otherwise, you are just another fat cat.

Of course, you can't do anything that appears to be an attempt to buy good coverage. No passing out of baseball tickets! And when you do have lunch with a reporter, pick an unpretentious place. The reporter is going to have to pay, and she will be relieved not to have to explain a fancy tab to her bosses.

When it comes to the press, while you don't have to say yes to everything, aloof is a bad idea. If you are only available to a reporter when you have a positive story to get out, that's like only being available for a Saturday night date. If you're not available to help move the couch, it is not a relationship. A reporter who has no relationship with you will have no compunction about ruining your reputation.

> IF YOU ARE ONLY AVAILABLE TO A REPORTER WHEN YOU HAVE A POSITIVE STORY TO GET OUT, THAT'S LIKE ONLY BEING AVAILABLE FOR A SATURDAY NIGHT DATE.

REGULATORS AND PROSECUTORS—MORE COPS PATROLLING MORE ALERTLY

Regulators and their close allies in the offices next door, the prosecutors, have long had a lot of power over big organizations. Until recently, however, they didn't use it often.

But two important things happened to change that. First, federal regulators, particularly the Securities and Exchange Commission, were embarrassed in 2002 to have been caught snoozing while enormous accounting frauds and stock research scandals brewed.

At the same time, Eliot Spitzer, then New York State's attorney general, took it upon himself to use some underemployed old laws to bring securities analysts, mutual funds, and insurance industry players to heel.

Now the federal agencies have woken up. The SEC hired hundreds of new lawyers, accountants, and investigators in the wake of those giant accounting frauds. Before his fall from grace, Spitzer's career inspired state regulators everywhere, who now think, "Hey, I can be famous, too." Even cities are getting into the act. In early 2008, Cleveland and Baltimore both sued banks for their role in the subprime mortgage meltdown.

In other words, there are a lot more compliance sheriffs in town than there used to be—and they are a lot more ambitious. Attract the attention of one, and you may attract the attention of many. Don't think you can escape their attention just because you are in the nonprofit or academic world, either. New York's next attorney general after Spitzer, Andrew Cuomo, won a series of nice headlines for himself in 2007 by going after university financial aid departments for taking kickbacks from student loan companies.

Because they are more active, regulatory agencies can attract better people, too—so they are now full of smart young men and women hoping to make a career on your stupidity or cupidity.

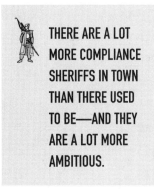 THERE ARE A LOT MORE COMPLIANCE SHERIFFS IN TOWN THAN THERE USED TO BE—AND THEY ARE A LOT MORE AMBITIOUS.

This is a very tough crowd. In my opinion, deep down, many of them believe that corporations, big nonprofits, and universities are inherently arrogant and corrupt—and it's just a question of finding out what's corrupt about *you*. You do not want to get caught in this vortex. So how to handle them?

The first rule is the same as that for reporters: Develop relationships with your regulators before there is trouble on the horizon. Hire lawyers who've worked as regulators and understand their motivations. Have people on your staff who know the top people in the regulators' offices.

Whenever possible, get to know these people yourself. Leave your plush tower and visit their spare government offices just to introduce yourself. Encourage them to call you personally if they need anything. Regulators are often forced to pass judgment on industries they have never worked in and may not understand very well. As a result, they may welcome your advice now and then.

DEVELOP RELATIONSHIPS WITH YOUR REGULATORS BEFORE THERE IS TROUBLE ON THE HORIZON.

If your regulators know you, you are far less likely to become a political target down the road. And if you do ever find your organization a subject of interest—and need three weeks to prepare the paperwork that will answer the regulators' questions—you will probably get the time.

What if you discover that there is a problem in your organization that could draw the attention of regulators?

Fix it.

If you manufacture chocolate and somebody in your organization worries that there may be mouse droppings in one batch, recall all the chocolate. Don't wait for the chocolate to be tested. Foot-dragging is something regulators won't stand for.

LEAVE YOUR PLUSH TOWER AND VISIT THEIR SPARSE GOVERNMENT OFFICES JUST TO INTRODUCE YOURSELF.

If a scandalous story hits the newspapers before you can discuss it with your regulators, you are, by definition, on the defensive. Ideally, get out in front of your regulators whenever possible and work with them to solve any problem.

For example, when I was at John Hancock, we had somebody working for us who sold an inappropriate product to a lot of Boston police officers. As soon as we discovered this, I asked for a meeting with the mayor and the police commissioner. I assured them that we would analyze every case individually and make every police officer whole.

Now, the mayor and the police commissioner are busy people. If I hadn't already made an effort to get to know them, I might not have gotten that meeting.

What did it help us avoid? Possibly criminal action, a lawsuit, fines, and some really awful newspaper headlines, any one of which can be a career killer.

The goal here is not to get your regulators to look the other way if you have done something truly egregious. That is not going to happen. If you've deliberately poured toxic waste into the river for 25 years, forget it. If, however, there has merely been an undetected leak, you may get a chance to fix the problem without being punished severely.

The goal here is to win the benefit of the doubt in the gray areas.

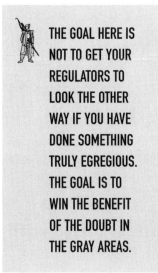

THE GOAL HERE IS NOT TO GET YOUR REGULATORS TO LOOK THE OTHER WAY IF YOU HAVE DONE SOMETHING TRULY EGREGIOUS. THE GOAL IS TO WIN THE BENEFIT OF THE DOUBT IN THE GRAY AREAS.

WALL STREET ANALYSTS—THE FIX MAY BE IN

During the dot-com boom, stock analysts at brokerage houses often gave investors an unrealistically enthusiastic picture of the stocks they covered. There was a purpose to this good cheer, of course. It helped their firms win investment banking business from those same companies.

Then Eliot Spitzer got interested in this conflict of interest, and there were public hangings, big fines, and some new rules. Now analysts have discovered a new power—to talk a stock down—and this has only increased their influence over the companies they cover.

And while the post-Spitzer rules have clamped down on some conflicts, one obstacle to the analyst's objectivity is never going to disappear: They make predictions about the future performance of your stock, and it's in their interest to do everything they can to turn those predictions into self-fulfilling prophecies.

ANALYSTS ARE A BIT LIKE TOUTS AT THE RACE TRACK. IF THEY PICK SIX OUT OF NINE WINNERS, THEY GAIN REPUTATION. INEVITABLY, THEY WILL BE TEMPTED TO FIX THE RACE.

They are a bit like touts at the race track. If they pick six out of nine winners, they gain reputation. So, if they want to be named "analyst of the year" and wear the tuxedo to the banquet, they have to be right.

Inevitably, they will be tempted to fix the race. To accomplish this, they have a few tools. They have the power of their own platforms and their ability to write forceful reports that will move a stock up or down. They can also draw the attention of the press to your brilliant moves or shortcomings. And they can use their earnings estimates to set the bar absurdly high for you—or condescendingly low—and influence your stock's performance in that way.

Since many investment strategies allocate certain dollars to certain industries, in the short term, they are playing a zero-sum game. If they prefer one of your competitors, it is just as effective to talk you down as to whip your competitor up. So you may very well find yourself covered by a certain percentage of analysts who are die-hard critics.

The fact is, if you work for a public company, you cannot ignore the analysts who cover you. They have tremendous power. So how do you handle them?

First, acknowledge that power. Make sure that your organization has excellent investor relations people who are respected by the analysts who follow your industry.

Second, you must be prepared to make your case to the analysts. At John Hancock, we had analysts attack us on a number of issues, and they often simply had the facts wrong. So give them the correct facts.

Third, don't try to hide your mistakes. If you are wrong and an analyst is right, then get out in front of it and admit, "Yes, we blew this one." This way, you may convert those analysts who don't like your stock.

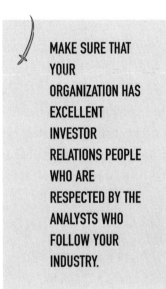

MAKE SURE THAT YOUR ORGANIZATION HAS EXCELLENT INVESTOR RELATIONS PEOPLE WHO ARE RESPECTED BY THE ANALYSTS WHO FOLLOW YOUR INDUSTRY.

Of course, some analysts are not convertible. And being on the spit at meetings and on conference calls, only to be probed by them, is not a lot of fun. I've listened to thousands of analyst conference calls over the years, and I've heard a number of CEOs and CFOs blow their cool under pressure. Generally, they call the analyst some form of nincompoop.

This is not recommended. Sure, you'll get a few "attaboys" in the company cafeteria afterward, but you will pay for it. Not only will there be investors listening in who may then rethink your stock, but the other analysts will now swarm as if you've attacked the whole hive. Worst of all, you've just enhanced the nincompoop analyst's reputation, since it's a badge of honor among analysts to ask such probing questions that management gets ticked off. There is no upside to getting personal with analysts.

THERE IS NO UPSIDE TO GETTING PERSONAL WITH ANALYSTS.

On the other hand, I don't believe in simply lying down, either. At one meeting, an analyst was so eager to argue with me about our Internet strategy that I had to point out to him that the sign onstage said this was a Q&A, not a debate. I'd answered his question and a few follow-ups, and now we were done. "If you own our stock, I'd advise you to sell it because you are so unhappy," I added.

The truth is that people want to own the stocks of companies that are run by leaders. Not by people who are afraid of analysts, not by people who are temperamental and blow up at them, but by people able to show some composure when questioned.

The one thing you must never, ever do with analysts is succumb to the pressure to meet their consensus earnings estimates for your company.

 PEOPLE WANT TO OWN THE STOCKS OF COMPANIES THAT ARE RUN BY LEADERS. NOT BY PEOPLE WHO ARE AFRAID OF ANALYSTS, NOT BY PEOPLE WHO ARE TEMPERAMENTAL AND BLOW UP AT THEM, BUT BY PEOPLE ABLE TO SHOW SOME COMPOSURE WHEN QUESTIONED.

This consensus represents one of the more counterproductive ways Wall Street tries to influence public companies' managements. The number is a bit like a fruitcake assembled without a recipe. Nobody is quite sure how much candied lemon peel is in it.

The people who contribute to it are inevitably a mixed bag. There may be 30 analysts following your company, of whom only 40 percent will follow you closely and actually do the analytical work to evaluate you.

The other 60 percent follow you only enough to write generally about you and to offer an annual consensus number. Yet they are also eligible to participate in the average—with their annual numbers prorated for the quarter.

In addition, these estimates are by no means always the analysts' best guesses. An analyst may make his or her earnings projections deliberately high, knowing full well that you won't reach them and that your stock will be punished for it. Another analyst may set expectations deliberately low to dampen your stock price immediately. And sometimes the analysts who really like your stock will moderate their estimates just to keep the average down so that you can beat it.

THE CONSENSUS EARNINGS ESTIMATE IS A BIT LIKE A FRUITCAKE ASSEMBLED WITHOUT A RECIPE. NOBODY IS QUITE SURE HOW MUCH CANDIED LEMON PEEL IS IN IT.

As a result, parts of the consensus will be scientific, parts of it will be entirely political, and parts of it will be lazy tarot card reading. It's a meaningless number, yet your stock will suffer if you don't meet it, even by a penny a share.

But what *is* a penny a share? In rough terms, if you have 250 million outstanding shares, a penny a share represents a mere $2.5 million in net income. If you are making $250 million a quarter, that is just 1 percent of the total.

Arranging your business so predictably, down to the tiniest sliver, to match the consensus estimate quarter after quarter without cheating is impossible because of the pin-the-tail-on-the-donkey way the number is constructed.

Any company that hits its mark quarter after quarter is managing its earnings. And the consequences of that, as we well know, look like a *Law & Order* episode.

My advice is, give Wall Street proper warning, but miss your numbers when you need to. It's better than joining Jeff Skilling and Bernie Ebbers in prison.

THE EXPECTATION OF WEALTH—DON'T BE A LEMMING

The pressures that Wall Street puts on organizations to make their numbers, come hell or high water, may someday lead your bosses to put pressure on you. Word may come down from on high that you need to alter your books slightly; some expense in your area ought to be reclassified or ignored.

You may be inclined to be a good sport and just make the change. After all, your day is probably so tied up in your organization that it's easy to forget that there are outside rules.

Even worse, much of your personal wealth may be tied up in your organization, too, whether it's $100,000 or $100 million, thanks to the rise of equity-based compensation for executives. The lure of using some little trick to prop up your company's share price can be overwhelming. This is especially true if you own a lot of stock options that will be underwater if the share price declines, or if you have been so foolish as to borrow against your stock.

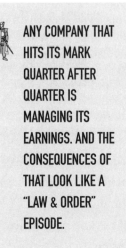

ANY COMPANY THAT HITS ITS MARK QUARTER AFTER QUARTER IS MANAGING ITS EARNINGS. AND THE CONSEQUENCES OF THAT LOOK LIKE A "LAW & ORDER" EPISODE.

It's also easy to minimize this kind of accounting manipulation to yourself. Maybe the expense you are supposed to reclassify or not record is relatively small, say $2 million.

The problem is that if you are being ordered to do such a thing, it's an excellent bet that so is every one of your peers without your being aware of it. If there are 30 divisions in your organization making similar changes, that's $60 million. If the company can't make that $60 million up in the next quarter and the tricks continue quarter after quarter, before you know it, the total is hundreds of millions of dollars, which will probably never be made up. That is how accounting scandals snowball. It's like your mother told you: Steal a penny, you'll soon be stealing a dollar.

So do not give in to this temptation to prop up the stock price at all costs. We didn't at John Hancock. If you behave like a lemming and toddle off the cliff with all your peers, your personal wealth may wind up at zero minus the money you spend defending yourself in court.

Perversely enough, however, it's difficult to rid yourself of this temptation by diversifying your investments. That's because Wall Street frowns on insiders selling any stock. The irony of this came into sharp focus for me once at a cocktail party when a big investor came over to me. "Stand here," he said to me. "I want to get my wife."

He brought her over. "This is David D'Alessandro. He has made us rich three times." From the time we had our IPO to the last day of trading before our merger with Manulife Financial closed—slightly over four years—John Hancock's stock went from $17 a share to $43.75.

The reason he'd said *three times* is that he'd moved in and out of the stock that often, selling on the rises. Meanwhile, he was the first guy to complain if any of my executives sold a share. "They're losing confidence in the company," he'd wail.

> THE LURE OF USING SOME LITTLE TRICK TO PROP UP YOUR COMPANY'S SHARE PRICE CAN BE OVERWHELMING, ESPECIALLY IF YOU OWN A LOT OF STOCK OPTIONS THAT WILL BE UNDERWATER IF THE SHARE PRICE DECLINES.

I always endorsed the idea that if you want to sell the stock, sell the stock. You're certainly a lemming if you participate in any trickery to boost your organization's stock price, so don't be a lemming when it comes to your stock holdings, either. Cash out when you can. Reap the benefits of your hard work all along the way, because nobody can live on paper wealth.

If the value of your company stock plummets overnight—as it did in 2008 for the employees of Bear Stearns during the subprime mortgage meltdown—you'll soon discover that paper has no nutritional value whatsoever.

BOARDS—AN OLD BOSS WITH A NEW MOOD . . . PARANOID

Since the great scandals of recent history, lots of new rules have been put in place for public companies surrounding the independence of their board members. While boards are no longer stuffed with insiders, that doesn't mean that the types of people who serve on these boards have changed all that much. It's not as if everyone who comes to board meetings now is wearing Birkenstocks. They still wear ties and wingtips and appropriate Hillary Clinton–like pantsuits. They may not come straight from the organization's club, but they are still plenty clubby.

IT'S LIKE YOUR MOTHER TOLD YOU: STEAL A PENNY, YOU'LL SOON BE STEALING A DOLLAR.

What has changed, however, is the lens through which board members view the executives they oversee. Directors all over America watched the boards of Enron and WorldCom pull money out of their own pockets to settle securities class-action lawsuits—and shivered. More frightening to directors even than a financial hit is a reputational hit—such as the one Home Depot's well-respected cofounder Kenneth Langone took after defending outsized pay packages for former New York Stock Exchange chief Richard Grasso and former Home Depot chief Bob Nardelli.

I ALWAYS ENDORSED THE IDEA THAT IF YOU WANT TO SELL THE STOCK, SELL THE STOCK.

"What about me?" your directors are now always thinking. "Could I get in trouble if I agree to this decision? If I place my trust in this particular executive?"

They are far less likely now to take any risk that may come back to haunt them—unless, of course, their paranoia deteriorates into a witch hunt, as it clearly did at Hewlett-Packard in 2005 and 2006. There, former chairman Patricia Dunn was so upset by leaks to the press that she author-ized a highly unusual, if not illegal, secret investigation of her fellow direc-tors and reporters that included accessing their private phone records and putting tracers on their e-mails. This particular moment of obsessiveness ended in a Congressional hearing.

The paranoid mood is one reason that I don't serve on public company boards anymore despite having been asked many times. Boards are now bogged down in minutiae. They no longer spend their time helping to run the company but instead spend it ensuring that proper procedures are followed, that the reports are correct, and that the i's are dotted and the t's are crossed.

If you want to rise in this new environment, you have to be reassuring to these nervous Nellies. You have to go the extra mile now to appear to be a responsible executive who will not get your directors in trouble. The mere suspicion of a problem is a taint that you can't get rid of now.

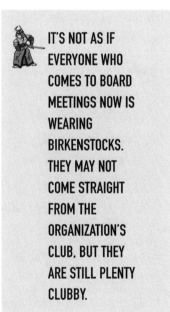

IT'S NOT AS IF EVERYONE WHO COMES TO BOARD MEETINGS NOW IS WEARING BIRKENSTOCKS. THEY MAY NOT COME STRAIGHT FROM THE ORGANIZATION'S CLUB, BUT THEY ARE STILL PLENTY CLUBBY.

As soon as your name is raised for a promotion, a director may ask, "Didn't we have an investigation of a financial irregularity in his area a few years ago?"

Even if nothing was found, suddenly there is a pig on the table. It may not oink, but that pig has your name on it.

If there really is a problem or a lag in your performance, you are more likely to be thrown on a sacrificial fire these days than at any other time in modern history. A recent Booz Allen study found that, in 1995, only one out of eight CEOs who left their organizations did so because they were forced out; by 2006, it was one out of three.

If you are thrown on that fire, you may not rise from it like a phoenix because the entire organizational world is so much less forgiving than it used to be—and less forgiving because of fright.

None of this should make you risk-averse, however. It should just make you a little more careful not to overpromise, not to carry dead weight in your operation, and not to go near anything that might embarrass your directors.

THE NEW OWNERS—DELIVER FOR THESE PEOPLE OR PREPARE TO VACATE

In this new climate, the people who invest in your organization, whether as owners or as donors, are much more active and aggressive than they used to be. We've become a culture of people who expect and demand high returns—boomers saving for their retirements, Gen-Xers ready to move to a bigger house, and billionaires trying to lead a green revolution or eradicate a disease.

> BOARDS ARE NOW BOGGED DOWN IN MINUTIAE. IF YOU WANT TO RISE IN THIS NEW ENVIRONMENT, YOU HAVE TO BE REASSURING TO THESE NERVOUS NELLIES.

To be successful, executives have to listen to these demands. But they also have to draw the line at certain kinds of interference from their investors and do what's best for the organization.

In my opinion, former Home Depot CEO Bob Nardelli clearly drew the line in the wrong place in 2006, at an annual meeting where the shareholders had lots of questions for the board about the stagnating stock price and Nardelli's compensation. Only there were no other board members present besides Nardelli, and according to *New York Times* reporter Joe Nocera, who attended, "the now-deposed Home Depot chief executive refused to answer so much as a single question from shareholders."

There were also digital clocks at the front of the stage that counted down the brief amount of time that each shareholder was allowed to speak. Nocera notes, "In the meeting's aftermath, the timers became a symbol of the authoritarian, contemptuous way he had treated shareholders. They surely hastened his demise."

In an open forum like this, you must be gracious and not too thin-skinned to respond to tough questions.

Be careful, however, with investors whose agendas do not match the agendas of your other donors or shareholders. The rise of hedge funds is dangerous for executives because hedge fund managers are generally not interested in holding the stock for a long time—only in making a quick killing.

WE'VE BECOME A CULTURE OF PEOPLE WHO EXPECT AND DEMAND HIGH RETURNS.

Depending on whether those hedge fund managers are taking a long or short position in your company, it's in their interest to push your stock up or down. And they have the clout to do it. They may buy just enough stock to come to meetings and question you so that they can make the rest of your audience uneasy.

Or they can talk to the press and spread false rumors about you. Is this legal? No. Does it happen? Yes. These fictions can play havoc with your stock, but I don't believe in giving in to market manipulators. As CEO of John Hancock, I generally refused to see anybody who owned less than three percent of the company. I rarely met with hedge fund managers, preferring that they sell the stock instead.

Of course, you may be out of this game entirely, thanks to one of the private equity firms that have bought public companies at an astounding clip in recent years. A private equity owner can help you to escape some of the perversities of the stock market, as well as some of the regulatory scrutiny and compliance burdens of being a public company.

At the same time, get used to a new kind of scrutiny. Your board will now be made up of big investors in your organization, and they are not going to just sit back and enjoy the occasional show-and-tell from you. They are looking for very high returns and will not wait 10 years for your strategy to play out in order to get them. Instead, they will dip into your business. They will send their own teams in to second-guess you. If you are used to being in charge, this interference may be difficult to bear.

There are some very good private equity players, and there are some awful ones. The good ones have run businesses and really know how to improve a company's performance. But there are other private equity people who have never led anything except for a fraternity party. They are simply financial engineers who want to slice up your organization or flip it to one of your competitors as fast as possible.

> THERE ARE SOME VERY GOOD PRIVATE EQUITY PLAYERS, AND THERE ARE SOME AWFUL ONES WHO HAVE NEVER LED ANYTHING EXCEPT FOR A FRATERNITY PARTY.

When you're in that whirlpool, you have one of two choices: Either develop an exit strategy, or make sure that you are capable of delivering the returns these owners demand.

Interestingly enough, something equivalent to the rise of private equity is happening at many nonprofits, too. This has been called a "golden age of philanthropy," thanks to the emergence of civic-minded billionaires around the world, but it's also a golden age of privatization. The world's wealthiest people are now taking on challenges like public schools and public health that were once the sole purview of government. And if you are an executive at a nonprofit, you may well find government support for your efforts dropping as a percentage of the whole, thanks to big contributions by super-wealthy donors.

These new philanthropists expect to improve lives on a sweeping scale. And they are not content just to write checks. They are applying their business smarts to their charitable work, too. As Rockefeller Foundation President Judith Rodin told *Fortune* about Bill and Melinda Gates, "They care deeply, deeply, deeply about making a difference, but they don't get starry-eyed. They demand impact."

With bosses like this, you cannot afford to be complacent. You must deliver results.

EVERYBODY WITH AN INTERNET CONNECTION— YOU ANSWER TO THEM, TOO

While new information technologies have been great for business and have enabled smart executives to reach out to their customers in much more compelling ways, they have also given many more people influence over executives' careers than most of them would like.

When it comes to the Internet, it is still surprising to me how many executives do not grasp the immediate power of information transfer. In just my own career I've seen a transformation from the time when only five people got the memo because that's as deep as a carbon would go. Then the Xerox machine became commonplace, and hundreds of people could be handed a copy. Then word processors arrived, and you could pump out as many drafts of as many memos as you wanted and send them through fax machines.

WHEN YOU'RE IN THAT WHIRLPOOL, EITHER DEVELOP AN EXIT STRATEGY, OR MAKE SURE THAT YOU ARE CAPABLE OF DELIVERING THE RETURNS THESE OWNERS DEMAND.

Then came the Internet and e-mail. Now anybody can instantly send the memo to anybody around the world or make it publicly accessible on a Web site. This is what allowed al Qaeda to thrive even after losing its home base in Afghanistan in 2001.

Unfortunately, there are lots of business terrorists lurking out there, too. People who will use whatever they find on you in order to embarrass you, sue you, or prosecute you.

It never ceases to amaze me that executives continue to think that when they communicate digitally, these communications are as private as those carbon-paper memos once were. Or that they are anonymous—as if leaving your name off an e-mail or a post were the equivalent of flipping a stranger the bird on the highway. Or that they are as ephemeral as the spoken word. As a lawyer I respect once told me, "Hard drives last *forever.*" That ought to be a mantra for senior executives.

 THERE ARE LOTS OF BUSINESS TERRORISTS LURKING OUT THERE—PEOPLE WHO WILL USE WHATEVER THEY FIND ON YOU IN ORDER TO EMBARRASS YOU, SUE YOU, OR PROSECUTE YOU.

It's been shown over and over that sending any message electronically is tantamount to publishing it. As New York State's attorney general, Eliot Spitzer was able to bring down target after target with incriminating e-mails. One prosecutor in Spitzer's office called e-mails "the functional equivalent of eavesdropping." *New York Magazine* also reported that Spitzer's office used law students to go through the e-mails that would help to build its bid-rigging case against insurance broker Marsh & McLennan. It was that easy.

E-mails can cause you a world of trouble within your organization, too. There was an executive at John Hancock, for example, who once wrote a scathing memo about a peer. Scathing. But instead of hitting "Reply," to send it to the person she trusted, she hit "Reply all," publishing her animosity throughout the company. This was a mess to be unscrambled, and it did not do wonderful things for her career.

I not only refused to send anything electronically that I wouldn't want to see in an analyst's report, but I also strongly discouraged other people from e-mailing me gossip or personal information. If something inappropriate fell into my hands, I would not even finish it. Instead, I would send it to the legal department.

Investor chat rooms and blogs are equally bad places to let your guard down. I do think it's important to know what's being said about you. If necessary, hire an outsider to comb the Web for mentions of your name. And if there are misconceptions, find an above-board way to correct them.

But don't wade into the fray yourself. When terrible things appeared on the Web about me and my company, I used to want to argue, too. So I understand the temptation to flame somebody and hit the "Send" key. You're being called a pirate, and you think, "Oh, I could defend myself anonymously; I could hide."

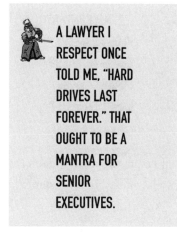 A LAWYER I RESPECT ONCE TOLD ME, "HARD DRIVES LAST FOREVER." THAT OUGHT TO BE A MANTRA FOR SENIOR EXECUTIVES.

Ultimately, you can't. John Mackey, the cofounder and CEO of Whole Foods, learned this the hard way. For years, he posted on Yahoo! Finance message boards under an alias, sometimes disparaging rival organic grocery chain Wild Oats. Then, when Whole Foods decided to acquire Wild Oats in 2007, documents that the company released to the Federal Trade Commission inadvertently revealed his Yahoo! identity. Though Whole Foods eventually prevailed, Mackey clearly did not improve his case with the FTC, which tried to block the merger on the grounds that it was anticompetitive. He also provoked both an independent internal investigation and an SEC inquiry.

Mackey's reasons for doing something so foolhardy? According to both the *Wall Street Journal* and the *New York Times*, his initial explanation was this: "I posted on Yahoo! under a pseudonym because I had fun doing it."

The casualness of self-expression that the Internet encourages is quite dangerous. *Wired* magazine's Clive Thompson may argue for business leaders to engage in "radical transparency" and communicate in an uncensored fashion online. But there is a difference between being fashionable and being smart. Obviously, there are many fantastic ways to use the Web for business, including offering detailed product information and interactive customer service, even interactive marketing that harnesses the creativity of your customers to sell your products. But, unless you want to spend a good portion of your life in depositions, I don't see letting fly in a company blog as a very smart move for rising executives.

> **UNLESS YOU WANT TO SPEND A GOOD PORTION OF YOUR LIFE IN DEPOSITIONS, I DON'T SEE LETTING FLY IN A COMPANY BLOG AS A VERY SMART MOVE FOR RISING EXECUTIVES.**

Thompson is right about one thing, though, when he writes, "Google is not a search engine. Google is a reputation-management system. . . . Online, your rep is quantifiable, findable, and totally unavoidable." I'd only add that it can be ruined in an instant.

Any embarrassment you allow to be captured in electronic form can spread like a virus and linger forever. So, when in doubt, don't do anything in front of the world's Google users that you wouldn't do in front of your organization's CEO and board.

A NEW WORLD FOR EXECUTIVES— TOUGH BUT NOT INHUMAN

The new world I have just described is more analytical, more numbers-focused, more aggressive, more skeptical, and more unforgiving than ever before. You have to be effective in this world to make it to the top—but the real stand-out candidates will be the amateur psychologists, the humanists, and the humorists.

That's because the information age has brought power to so many new constituencies who never had much before. The executives best able to manage relationships with these different constituencies are the ones who will wind up running the organizations—and reaping the benefits, including high-end compensation.

If you want to rise, you have to demonstrate leadership to many different audiences. These include the people above and below you in the organizational hierarchy, the people who are competing with you for the next job and those resentful because they cannot compete for it, the outsiders and insiders and shareholders and donors and disinterested observers only looking for a juicy story to alleviate the tedium.

You will never convince all these different audiences to trust you if you don't have a very strong sense of yourself and a good idea of what integrity is. But you also have to listen to all these bosses, think about them, and try to understand their agendas.

In today's world, you have to be alert to win.

AFTERWORD

Bring Heat and Light To the Room

Presence is more than just being there.

Malcolm Forbes

I was once having dinner with a board member at a large and important organization, and we were nearing the end of the main course. I've had enough experience at business dinners to know that the moment of truth always occurs when you're finishing up the entrée. People don't tell you what's on their minds over cocktails or the appetizer, for fear of making things awkward when there's still a lot of evening left to slog through. In my opinion, business dinners would be a lot cheaper and more efficient if everybody just ordered an entrée and got to the point.

Anyway, as our plates were being cleared, this director let me know that he was worried about his organization's succession plan and wanted my opinion. There were three possible candidates to succeed the CEO, and he was torn. One had great financial skills, another one was great at marketing, and the third was good with people. To him, it was a real dilemma.

IF YOU WANT TO RISE INTO THE SENIOR RANKS IN YOUR ORGANIZATION—OR DO THE HARDER THING, WHICH IS STAY THERE—YOU MUST BECOME A PERSON OF PRESENCE.

I said, "The choice is easy. Who is the room-changer? Which one creates a dramatically different and more positive aura whenever he or she walks into the room? Even if your back is to the door, you don't need trumpets or 'Hail to the Chief' to know that a person of presence has come in.

"That one," I continued, "is the leader, the one who is comfortable with himself or herself, the one who won't be afraid to make the right decisions. That's the CEO you want."

If you want to rise into the senior ranks in your organization—or do the harder thing, which is stay there—you must become a person of presence. This is the underlying quality we have been talking about throughout this book.

How do you get to be that person of presence? First of all, you have to offer something substantial and not just self-importance. When I was first a senior executive, I visited a fellow executive perched in an office very high up in a Manhattan skyscraper. It was 4:30 in the afternoon, and the building faced due west, offering an unobscured view of the sunset. When I stepped into this office, the executive was getting ready for a meeting. He wasn't lowering the blinds, as you'd expect, to protect his visitors from the glare. No, he was raising them and then rearranging the furniture so his back would be to the window.

He explained what he was doing: "When I'm negotiating something, I want people to understand that they are in a powerful place. This way, they won't be able to see me. I'll be a shadow. They'll only hear my voice and know that they are with a very powerful person."

IF YOU TRY TO CRAFT A PERSONALITY OR STYLE OUT OF THIN AIR, YOU WON'T LAST. YOU WILL BE INCONSISTENT, MAKE MISTAKES.

More like, with a moron. His idea of how to express power was one of the dumbest things I've ever heard. If he wanted his negotiating guests to understand that he was somebody to be reckoned with, the heat and light should have been coming from him, not from the window behind him.

He should have made it vividly clear that he possessed the energy to listen to a proposal, solve a problem, and make things happen. That is power. It comes not only from your authority but also from your ability to establish your presence. After that, I never put my back to a window in a meeting when I controlled the environment.

Second, to be a person of presence, you have to be true to yourself and the things you believe. If you try to craft a personality or style out of thin air, you won't last. You will be inconsistent, make mistakes. Even those people who do stick to their principles make enemies. But you will make many, many more if you are fickle in your thinking or behavior—and people will not follow you or respect you.

When you do take a position on any organizational issue, you should be as careful and as certain of what you are doing as anybody high up in politics has to be. The classic political advice, "Think of how it will look in a 30-second attack ad," is worth keeping in mind, no matter what your business. At this level, if you flip-flop too many times, you will lose your constituency—and your ability to move up.

The third thing it takes to become a person of presence is perspective—and you cannot develop perspective if your entire life revolves around your job.

Though it's contrary to some conventional wisdom about how to succeed, I highly recommend having interests outside the office—interests that you can pursue without people from the office. Don't take so much

> AS A TOP EXECUTIVE, YOU WILL BE LONELY IN MANY OF THE HOURS YOU SPEND AT WORK BECAUSE YOU HAVE TO MAKE SO MANY DECISIONS ON YOUR OWN. DON'T EXTEND THAT LONELINESS TO YOUR PERSONAL LIFE.

work home with you that you look like a donkey at the end of the day. Whether it's on your computer or in paper form, you probably won't look at it all anyway. Try to avoid speaking the Star Trek language of executives, which eliminates all emotion in favor of basis points, leverage, and click-through rates. Make friends who have nothing to do with your organizational life—and don't sacrifice your family for your job, no matter how important.

As a top executive, you will be lonely in many of the hours you spend at work because you have to make so many decisions on your own. Don't extend that loneliness to your personal life. Not only will it help your career if you have family and outside friends who can offer you advice and support—you also will not be a pathetic and unhappy figure when your career is over.

Keep a sense of humor, too, because there is plenty of absurdity at the top of any organization, and you will make better decisions if you recognize it.

Above all, avoid being isolated by your success. Most people are not interested in anarchy—they want to be led. But, they won't take their cues from someone out of touch, someone who lives in a business or social cocoon.

 MOST PEOPLE ARE NOT INTERESTED IN ANARCHY—THEY WANT TO BE LED. BUT THEY WON'T TAKE THEIR CUES FROM SOMEONE WHO LIVES IN A BUSINESS OR SOCIAL COCOON.

Once you crawl into that cocoon and start socializing only with people who are exactly like you, you still might rise, but you will not last. You simply won't know enough to survive the multifaceted challenges you'll inevitably face. It takes perspective to lead, and you can't get perspective on the sixteenth tee.

A lot of executives think that if they talk to the people whose paychecks they sign, they've stayed grounded. Well, I'm sorry, but those people can't afford to contradict you. It's much more instructive to go to a baseball game and have somebody completely disinterested spill beer on you and yell at you. If you worry that a cocoon is being spun around you, go watch a roofer work in the heat of the summer or a waitress in a busy coffee shop. As I was rising, I'd sneak out of the office once or twice a year and go to court on sentencing day, just to observe. Make sure that you never forget that most lives involve a lot of struggle, because people will not look up to you if you have no empathy for them.

To get to the top—and stay there—you need to be able to lead human beings. And, the only way to learn how to lead is to live.

INDEX

ABOUT THE AUTHORS

David F. D'Alessandro, former chairman and CEO of John Hancock Financial Services, is the bestselling author of two previous books, *Brand Warfare* and *Career Warfare*. He is also a guest columnist for the *Boston Globe* and a frequent guest commentator and guest host for CNBC on business and social issues. He serves as an advisor to both corporations and universities on business and branding strategies, and is a sought-after guest speaker on these topics, as well as topics related to professional and career development.

Michele Owens coauthored two previous bestsellers with David D'Alessandro, *Career Warfare* and *Brand Warfare*, which was named one of the best business books of 2001 by *Library Journal*. She was chief speechwriter for Governor William F. Weld of Massachusetts and a staff speechwriter for Governor Mario Cuomo of New York. Her articles have appeared in *O, The Oprah Magazine, Organic Gardening*, and *Elle*, and she is a cocreator of GardenRant.com.

STAND OUT FROM THE RANK AND FILE

With National Bestselling Author
David F. D'Alessandro

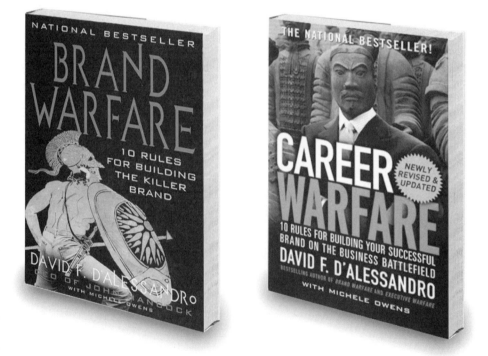

"D'Alessandro is that refreshing rarity:
A BUSINESSMAN WHO TELLS IT LIKE IT IS."
—Chicago Sun-Times